Foundations of
Ethical Counseling

Donald A. Biggs, Ed.D., is Professor of Counseling Psychology and Student Development at the State University of New York at Albany. He received his doctoral degree from the University of California at Los Angeles. Dr. Biggs was formerly Professor of Educational Psychology and Assistant to the Vice President for Student Affairs at the University of Minnesota. He has also served as Fulbright Visiting Professor at the University of Aston, Birmingham, England. Dr. Biggs has authored or co-authored a number of articles, chapters, and books.

Donald H. Blocher, Ph.D., is Professor of Counseling Psychology at the State University of New York at Albany. He has held professorships at the University of Minnesota and the University of Western Ontario, and has been visiting professor at Utah State University, the University of Colorado, the University of British Columbia, and the University of Keele in the United Kingdom. He received his doctoral degree from the University of Minnesota. Dr. Blocher is past president of the Division of Counseling Psychology of the American Psychological Association. He has authored or co-authored several books, including *Developmental Counseling.* He is also the author of numerous journal articles and is a Fellow of the American Psychological Association.

Foundations of Ethical Counseling

Donald Biggs
Donald Blocher

with a Contribution by
Garth Sorenson and Lisa V. Kassoy

SPRINGER PUBLISHING COMPANY
New York

Copyright © 1987 by Springer Publishing Company, Inc.

Springer Publishing Company, Inc.
536 Broadway
New York, NY 10012

87 88 89 90 91 / 5 4 3 2 1

Library of Congress Cataloging-in-Publication Data

Biggs, Donald A.
  Foundations of ethical counseling.

  Bibliography: p.
  Includes index.
  1. Counseling ethics.   I. Blocker, Donald H.
II. Title.
BF637·C6B445   1987   174'·915   86—33891
ISBN 0—8261—4960—X (soft)

Printed in the United States of America

Contents

Preface

This book deals with thinking and acting in the face of ethical problems and dilemmas. It examines the process of ethical growth and development. This process is an essential part of the preparation of every professional counselor.

This is a process that is not limited merely to reading textbooks, learning about ethical codes, or taking formal courses. Rather, ethical development is a deeply personal and totally involving process of confronting one's own values, commitments, and ways of thinking and feeling.

We, the authors, sincerely hope that this book will help to set in motion a set of ideas, values, and commitments that will start the reader on an exciting path of self-discovery and cognitive growth that can continue throughout a professional career.

To ensure that this growth pattern continues throughout the entire period of professional preparation and beyond, we urge readers to form "ethical development groups" in order to share the ethical challenges and confrontations that are found in practica, internships, and other preparation experiences.

To the extent that counselors are able to share perspectives, commitments, and values in a genuinely open and supportive way they are able to help each other grow and advance professionally and personally.

We see ethical counseling as a function of the clinician's quality of thinking and judging. Such thinking reflects an understanding of ethical codes, an examination of one's values, a consideration of one's philosophical beliefs, and most important, a willingness to explore and examine one's own cognitive processes.

We believe that the most important concept with which to begin the journey into ethical development is the notion of the dialectic, or constant interchange of ideas, perspectives, and values. The path of ethical development is not a quest for certainty but a road that leads to greater and greater appreciation of the complexity and diversity of human thinking and action.

When starting down the path, we encourage you to reflect on Nevitt Sanford's (1964) sage advice about the appropriate goals for higher education as you read this text:

> Higher education may be assigned other goals besides that of individual development, and it is possible to debate the relative importance of these goals. I put individual development first because in my view it is the most important goal in its own right. If you were to say it is more important that the individual be adjusted to his society, I would reply that it is more important that he be able to transcend and help to transform society. But I also argue that individual development should have first attention because it is favorable to the achievement of all other legitimate goals. Is it our aim to preserve culture? This can best be done by individuals who have been developed to a point where they can appreciate it. Do we wish to create culture? This is mainly done by highly developed individuals, although there are some important exceptions. Is it our desire to train people for vocations that require technical skills? If this can be done at all in college, it is through the development of qualities that are valuable in a great variety of jobs. Preparation for a high-level profession? Good performance in any profession depends heavily on qualities found only in highly developed individuals. Ask professors of engineering to characterize a good engineer, and they will list such qualities as leadership, capacity to make wise decisions, flexibility of thinking and so on. They ask how such characteristics are to be produced, and, receiving no answer, they go back to teaching mechanics and thermodynamics. (pp. 288–289)

This book focuses on the role of cognition in ethical counseling. Our approach is to encourage readers to examine the cognitive factors that can influence ethical counseling. The first section of this book primarily describes the cognitive components in the first two psychological processes in ethical counseling: (a) the interpretation and identification of ethical issues, and (b) the moral/ethical judgment process. In discussing the cognitive foundations of ethical counseling, we make a distinction between the cognitive content components in thinking, such as beliefs, and the cognitive structural components of thinking, such as "rules for thinking." Cognitive content variables represent the counselor's beliefs about professional ethics, such as knowledge of professional codes and standards, knowledge about various philosophical arguments for and against specific ethical criteria, and content of the counselor's values.

The second section of the book is entitled "Ethical Counseling: Professional Issues" and includes Chapter 5, which considers the ethical issues in clinical practice, and Chapter 6, which deals with ethical issues in assessment and research. The final section of the book is entitled "Cases in Ethical Counseling" and describes an approach to case analysis as well as a number of cases involving dilemmas in ethical counseling.

Over the years, counseling psychologists and counselors have grappled with questions regarding their professional identities. For a time, some of us even used the terms *counselor* and *counseling psychologist* interchangeably. However, with the growth of licensure and accreditation in psychology, there are increasing attempts to differentiate clearly the professional roles of counselors and counseling psychologists. Some of this activity has been helpful and has probably improved the quality of counseling services to clients. Still, the movement of counseling psychology away from the "Brethren in Counseling" and closer to the "Brethren in Psychology" sometimes appears to smack of elitism and discrimination. Counselors and counseling psychologists share a common heritage, and even today their roles in many agencies overlap. Thus, in this book we will refer to both counseling psychologists and counselors in discussing ethical counseling because we assume they share many common professional concerns, not because we necessarily consider them to play the same professional roles in all settings.

REFERENCES

Sanford, N. (1964). *College and character.* New York: John Wiley & Sons.

I
Cognitive Foundations of Ethical Counseling

The ultimate test of ethical prescriptions is not, however, conducted in the court of experience (even utilitarians think otherwise). Had Hitler's genocidal program been totally successful it would not thereby come to be judged as right. Nor would it have been right had all surviving non-Jews become somehow happier, or even if the victims had volunteered to be executed so that survivors would be happier. The ultimate test of ethical prescriptions is, alas, propositional, not empirical. The major premises of a moral argument are always subject to debate, which is why the discipline of moral philosophy is still alive. But once a given premise is granted (e.g., it is never right to take the life of an innocent, nonthreatening person), the balance of the argument unfolds with the certainty of a syllogism—because it is a syllogism. We need only supply the fact that Smith or Jones is, in fact, a nonthreatening and innocent person in order to conclude that *necessarily* it is not right to kill him.

—D. N. Robinson, *Ethics and Advocacy*

Chapter One
Introduction and Overview

ETHICS AND THE PROFESSIONAL ROLE

Ethical principles and ethical problems are an inevitable part of the professional life of counselors and counseling psychologists. They arise from the very nature of a profession itself. The term *professional* is hard to define. Definitions can be framed around criteria such as the number of years of preparation required, whether or not the professional engages in private or institutional practice, whether or not the profession is represented by formal groups or associations, and other similarly superficial considerations.

Professions arise out of a *public trust.* This trust defines the profession and permits the members of the professional group to function in professional ways. The public trust that creates and sustains any profession stems from three sets of beliefs that are widely held about the profession and its members.

Competence

Public trust begins with a perception of competence. Professionals are seen to have special expertise and competence not readily found in the general public. This competence is usually seen to arise out of specialized education and requirements for high levels of general and special abilities in order to complete that education. Usually, competence is formally attested to by both completion of formal preparation and by passing special examinations before entering professional practice. In some situations professionals may have to demonstrate continuing competence through periodic reexamination, continuing professional education, or other means.

Maintenance of Standards

The second perception that sustains public trust in a professional group is the belief that such groups both regulate themselves and are further regulated by society in the public interest. An important part of this perception is a faith in the codification of professional behavior. By codification of behavior we mean the existence of fairly clear and public standards and principles governing the professional's behavior. Members of the public can expect these standards to be observed and enforced. Further, it is expected that these standards and principles are clearly designed to protect the *public welfare*, not simply to enrich or enhance the professionals themselves.

Another aspect of this perception is the belief that members of the profession will organize and work to uphold prescribed standards of professional conduct. In other words, it is the belief that professionals will accept responsibility for policing themselves. An important characteristic of any profession is that it has two major mechanisms of self-regulation: the first is its self-generated code of ethics, and the second is its standards of practice (Jacobs, 1976).

Altruistic Values

The final perception from which a public trust is given is that members of a profession are motivated to serve the people with whom they work. This belief is perhaps the most fragile of the public perceptions on which trust is given. It is the faith that the professional is committed to values that transcend his or her own personal or monetary interests and that professional behavior will be guided by such values. These perceptions will be discussed in Chapter 5.

Ethical questions are rooted in the public trust that defines any profession, and that is the major reason that they are of central concern to *all* of the members of a professional group. Whenever the perceptions of the public are changed by the unethical, unprofessional, or irresponsible behavior of a member of the profession, all other members are harmed, and indeed their ability to function in professional ways is diminished or impaired.

Professionals who deliver counseling services must be especially concerned with ethical problems because their clients are often very vulnerable to manipulation and exploitation. Clients disclose very intimate issues in their lives and should be assured that such risk-taking will be respected and dealt with in a professional manner. We believe that ethical counseling should involve an awareness of and a commitment to maintain this important responsibility to protect client trust. The ethical counselor must be keenly aware of the possible impact of his or her actions on a client's present and future status and must be able to make complex moral/ethical judgments. Welfel and Lipsitz (1984), in a review of research about ethical behavior of psychologists, identified incidences of unethical behavior and practitioner characteristics associated with unethical behavior. They found that in general 5% to 10% of practitioners appear fairly insensitive to the ethical aspects of their work. However, they warn that the literature probably underrepresents the extent of the problem. We think that professionals who deliver counseling services need to be better prepared to analyze and make ethical judgments about the complex issues and dilemmas that will confront them in their professional lives.

PROFESSIONAL CODES OF ETHICAL STANDARDS

Two major professional organizations that affect counselors and counseling psychologists are the American Psychological Association (APA), in particular Division 17 (Counseling Psychology), and the American Association for Counseling and Human Development (AACD), formerly the American Personnel and Guidance Association. Both of these organizations have developed fairly elaborate ethical codes that they use as self-regulatory mechanisms. The value of these codes is that they can protect a profession from government interference, prevent internal disagreements within a profession, and protect practitioners in cases of alleged malpractice (Van Hoose & Kottler, 1985).

These professional codes of ethics are important knowledge variables and can influence the ethical judgments of counselors. The codes provide guidance regarding the ethical parameters of the profession.

APA ETHICS AND STANDARDS

The APA began largely as a scientific society focusing heavily on the advancement of psychology as a scientific discipline. After World War II the APA expanded its concerns to include the professional applications of psychology. Its more than 40 divisions now represent psychologists with very wide-ranging interests. The Division of Counseling Psychology represents counseling psychologists in a variety of professional matters. All members of the APA are bound by its ethical code.

The APA developed a comprehensive code of ethics in 1953. In 1959, they derived from the original code a set of 19 general principles that were adopted as the APA code in 1962. A revised code was adopted in 1979 that distilled these to nine principles.

The current ethical code of the APA, adopted in 1981, is the "Ethical Principles of Psychologists." The new statement included a tenth principle entitled "Care and Use of Animals" (the 1981 code can be found in Appendix A).

The 1981 ethical code involves the following ten principles:

1. Psychologists should maintain the highest standards of their profession, accept responsibility for the consequences of their acts, and ensure that their services are used appropriately.

2. Psychologists should provide only those services and use only those techniques for which they are qualified by training and experience.

3. Psychologists should be sensitive to the prevailing community standards, the possible impact of their public behavior on the quality of their performance as psychologists, and the impact such public behavior may have on their professional colleagues.

4. Psychologists should represent accurately and objectively their professional qualifications, affiliations, and functions as well as those of the institution with which they or their statements may be associated.

5. The fifth principle deals with the need to protect the confidentiality of information obtained from persons during the course of psychological treatment. This principle states that psychologists can reveal information obtained from a client only in cases where there is clear danger to the person or to others.

6. Psychologists should fully inform consumers as to the purpose and nature of an evaluation, treatment, or educational and training procedure, and they freely acknowledge that clients, students, or

participants in research have freedom of choice with regard to participation. Psychologists are neither to give nor to receive remuneration for referring clients for professional services.

7. Psychologists should understand and respect the areas of competence of related professions. For instance, psychologists do not directly offer their services to persons receiving similar services from another professional. Psychologists do not condone or engage in sexual harassment. Psychologists are cautioned about obtaining authorizations for doing research and assigning publication credit in proportion to professional contributions. Finally, a psychologist is to take responsible action if aware of any ethical violations by another psychologist.

8. In the development, publication, and utilization of psychological assessment techniques, psychologists should make every effort to promote the welfare and best interests of the client. They respect the client's right to know the results, interpretations, and bases for any conclusions.

9. Psychologists have the responsibility to make a careful evaluation of any research they undertake. The investigator must respect the individual's freedom to decline to participate in or to withdraw from a research project at any time. Except in minimal-risk research, the investigator should establish a clear and fair agreement with research subjects, prior to their participation, that clarifies the obligations and responsibilities of each.

10. Investigators will ensure the welfare of animals and treat them humanely. They are to make every effort to minimize the discomfort, illness, and pain of animals.

We will elaborate further on several of these principles in Chapter 5.

PROFESSIONAL STANDARDS FOR PROVIDERS OF PSYCHOLOGICAL SERVICES

In 1974, the APA first issued a policy statement entitled "Standards for Providers of Psychological Services." These standards give specific content to the profession's concept of ethical practice.

In 1977, the Standards were revised, and these represent the present standards for delivery of psychological services (the statement of these Standards can be found in Appendix B). The original Statement as well as the 1977 Statement reflect the following assumptions:

- A single set of standards should cover all types of psychologists in all manner of human service settings.
- A single generic definition of the psychologist qualified to offer independent services is to be based on holding an appropriate doctoral degree, the psychologist's academic qualifications, and appropriate experience.
- The same standards should govern provision of psychological services in both the private and public sectors.
- Psychologists should be strictly accountable to the standards but not constrained from using innovative methods and/or using support personnel.
- The standards should provide for changes in patterns of service delivery and should be open to review and revision.

The 1977 Standards can be summarized as follows:

The first standard deals with the qualifications of providers. There is a discussion of the roles of professional psychologists in a service-delivery organization, their need to maintain current knowledge in the field, and their need to limit their practice to demonstrated areas of competence.

The second standard deals with the composition and organization of a psychological services unit. There is a discussion of the need for programs to be responsive to the unique character of the persons and settings being served; the importance of having written documents that describe the organization, objectives, and scope of services; the need for adequate staffing; and the importance of protecting the civil and legal rights of users. When appropriate, a service-delivery unit is to have written procedural guidelines for delivery of services, written treatment plans, and accurate records that are secure and protect the confidentiality of the information.

The third standard deals with accountability and the promotion of human welfare. This standard discusses the need for psychologists to be aware of the implications of their activities for the profession as a whole and the importance of having periodic effective evaluations of services.

The fourth standard deals with the environment of the service unit. The social, the physical, and organizational environment of the service unit should facilitate the provision of high-quality services.

SPECIALTY GUIDELINES
FOR COUNSELING PSYCHOLOGISTS

Following the adoption of the generic standards for psychologists, the APA spent 3 years revising them to meet the needs of clinical, counseling, industrial/organizational, and school psychologists. In January 1980, the APA adopted the Specialty Guidelines for the Delivery of Services by Clinical, Counseling, Industrial/Organizational and School Psychologists.

These specialty guidelines for counseling psychologists, together with the generic standards, state the official policy of the APA regarding the delivery of services by counseling psychologists (the statement of these guidelines can be found in Appendix C). The intent of these guidelines was that psychologists were not to present themselves as specialists in counseling psychology unless they met the qualifications in the guidelines. One of the important functions of these specialty guidelines is that they provide content for a concept of ethical practice as it applies to the functions of counseling psychologists.

These guidelines define the professional counseling psychologist as an individual having a doctoral degree from a regionally accredited university or a professional school providing an organized, sequential counseling psychology program in an appropriate academic department in a university or college or in an appropriate academic department or unit of a professional school. Only individuals meeting the appropriate educational requirements should provide unsupervised counseling psychological services.

Counseling psychological services are a function of a counseling psychological services unit. The goals of such services should reflect a significant emphasis on the positive aspects of growth and adjustment. The counseling psychologists apply psychological principles, methods, and procedures to facilitate effective functioning during the life-span developmental process. The professional orientation is to be primarily developmental and preventive. The services are intended to help persons acquire or alter personal–social skills, improve adaptability to changing life demands, enhance environmental coping skills, and develop a variety of problem-solving and decision-making capabilities. Specific counseling services include (a) assessment, (b) individual and group interventions, (c) consultation, (d) program development, (e) supervision, and (f) evaluation. They are further discussed in Chapter 5.

THE AMERICAN ASSOCIATION
FOR COUNSELING AND DEVELOPMENT

The American Association for Counseling and Development (AACD) is another major professional organization that has a code of ethical standards that affects those professionals who deliver counseling services.

Although the first national conference for counselors was actually held more than 75 years ago, the development of professional organizations for counselors has been characterized by great diversity. The National Vocational Guidance Association was founded in 1913. Several of the early organizations representing counselors and personnel workers joined together in 1951 to form the American Personnel and Guidance Association. This organization changed its name in 1984 to become the American Association for Counseling and Development. All members are bound by the AACD ethical code.

AACD includes a number of divisions that are concerned with the delivery of counseling services in selected settings such as rehabilitation units, schools, colleges, prisons, employment offices, community mental units, and military services. Many of the counselors would have a master's degree as their terminal degree; however, some have the doctorate and some are also members of APA Division 17 (Counseling Psychology). In 1961, the American Personnel and Guidance Association adopted a statement of ethical standards, which was later revised in 1974. In 1981, the organization approved their present revision of their Code of Ethics. The statement includes a preamble and eight sections: (a) General, (b) Counseling Relationship, (c) Measurement and Evaluation, (d) Research and Publication, (e) Consulting, (f) Private Practice, (g) Personnel Administration, and (h) Preparation Standards (the statement of these standards can be found in Appendix D).

The general standards exhort AACD members to make continuous efforts to improve professional practices, teaching, services, and research. Members are to seriously consider terminating employment in any institutions where institutional policies are not conducive to the positive growth and development of clients. Members are also to take appropriate actions in those cases where they possess information that raises serious doubts about the ethical behavior of professional colleagues. Members neither claim nor imply professional qualifications exceeding those possessed, and they are personally responsible for correcting any misrepresentations. Finally, counselors are to be aware of the negative impact of both racial and sexual stereotyping and discrimination, and they are to protect clients from these influences.

The second section presents standards regarding the counseling relationship. Counselors are to recognize the need for client freedom of choice. Clients must be made aware of any conditions that might limit their freedom of choice. Confidentiality is to be maintained unless there is clear and imminent danger to the client or others. Counselors are to inform clients of the purposes, goals, techniques, rules of procedure, and limitations that may affect the relationship at or before the time that the counseling relationship is entered.

The third section of the standards deals with measurement and evaluation issues. Counselors are to provide specific orientation or information to the examinee(s) prior to and following the administration of tests so that the results can be placed in proper perspective with other relevant factors. They are also to consider specific validity, reliability, and appropriateness of tests. Unsupervised or inadequately supervised test-taking, such as the use of tests through the mails, is considered unethical.

The fourth section deals with research and publication issues. Counselors are to adhere to the statement of "Ethical Principles in the Conduct of Research with Human Participants" of the APA, as well as to the appropriate codes of federal regulations. Counselors, when conducting and reporting research, agree to be familiar with and give recognition to previous work on a topic, observe copyright laws, and give full credit to all to whom credit is due.

The section that deals with consulting issues defines consultation as a voluntary relationship between a professional helper and a help-needing individual, group, or social unit in which the consultant is providing help to the client(s) in defining and solving a work-related problem or potential problem with a client or client system. The purpose of the consulting relationship is to encourage and cultivate client adaptability and growth toward self-direction.

The section that deals with private practice standards encourages counselors to assist the profession by facilitating the development of counseling services in private as well as public settings. However, when advertising, counselors are to accurately list the following: the highest relevant degree, type and level of certification and license, type and/or description of services, and other relevant information. Such information should not contain false, inaccurate, misleading, partial, out-of-context, or deceptive material or statements.

The seventh section concerns issues regarding personnel administration and is concerned with preparation of professionals.

Faculty members are to be skilled as teachers and practitioners; they are to present varied theoretical positions and make students aware of the ethical responsibilities and standards of the profession.

THE COMPLAINT PROCESS

In the APA, the Committee on Scientific and Professional Ethics and Conduct (CSPEC) is responsible for adjudicating any complaints regarding violations of the ethical principles (Mills, 1984). The Committee consists of seven members chosen to reflect different specialties in psychology as well as different geographical areas. The Committee has jurisdiction over all Association members. They may dismiss a complaint as lacking substance, or reprimand or censure the member against whom the complaint was lodged. CSPEC typically conducts all of its business through correspondence, and the records of the Committee are such that the identity of individual complainants is protected.

The complaint process is initiated by sending a short letter to the Ethics Office at APA indicating that the person wishes to make a complaint against a particular individual. Later, the individual making the complaint is asked to supply the particulars. The committee does not investigate complaints between members if 1 year has elapsed from the time of the alleged incident. If the complaint is made by a nonmember against a member, the committee will investigate it if 5 years has not elapsed since the alleged infraction.

The next phase in the complaint process is the investigative stage. First, the person who is the subject of the complaint is notified and asked to make a response. After receiving all of the relevant information, a preliminary decision is made regarding the probable substance of the complaint.

The adjudication stage involves a review by the Ethics Committee in which it makes a decision regarding the case.

The committee can either dismiss the complaint as having no significant substance or it may reprimand or censure the member. The reprimand is for minor infractions, whereas the censure is more serious and usually involves stipulations such as going into treatment. The committee may negotiate with the member for his or her resignation. Finally, the Ethics Committee may recommend to the Board of Directors that a member be dropped or even expelled from membership. The person at whom the complaint is directed has 30 days to request an appeal. All appeals are heard by a Standing Hearing Panel of the Association.

The AACD Ethics Committee is a standing committee of the Association and consists of six appointed members including the chairperson. The Committee assists in the arbitration and conciliation of conflicts among members of the Association, where appropriate such nonmembers' client concerns may be expressed. All correspondence, records, and activities of the Ethics Committee are confidential.

The procedures of the AACD are similar to those of APA. In cases where a resolution of an ethical complaint is not forthcoming at the state level, the complainant must prepare a formal written statement of the complaint and submit it, witnessed by one AACD branch, to the AACD Executive Director or the Assistant Director for Association and Professional Relations. He or she checks on the membership status of the accused, confers with legal counsel, secures a legal opinion, and then sends the case to the chairperson of the Ethics Committee. The chair of the Ethics Committee will acknowledge receipt of the complaint to the complainant and ask the accused member for a response, including any relevant information concerning the complaint. After reviewing the information submitted by the accused member, the Ethics Committee may either dismiss the charges, request the accused member to voluntarily cease the practices without any sanctions, or impose sanctions. In some cases, the Ethics Committee may conduct hearings to gather additional information regarding a case. The burden of proving a violation of the ethical standards is on the complainant and/or the Committee.

The Ethics Committee is empowered to take any of the following disciplinary actions or sanctions: (a) issue a reprimand, (b) withdraw eligibility for membership in AACD for a specified time period, (c) place a member on probation, or (d) expel the accused from membership in AACD.

CONCLUSION

If counselors define themselves as professional persons, they need to assume the responsibility for improving the quality of their professional thinking and judgment about ethics. Based on this assumption, the present book discusses the cognitive components in ethical thinking and judgment of counselors.

The present chapter briefly described a major cognitive factor—

Cognitive Foundations of Ethical Counseling

knowledge of professional codes—that should influence the ethical thinking of counselors. The professional codes of two organizations, the APA and the AACD, were discussed. Interested readers are encouraged to read the professional codes of the National Association of Social Workers and the American Association for Marriage and Family Therapy.

In later chapters we will discuss applied issues in ethical counseling as well as provide a format for ethical analysis of cases. A number of cases will be used for such analyses.

REFERENCES

American Association for Counseling and Development. (1981). *Ethical standards.* Washington, DC: Author.
American Psychological Association. (1974). Rules and procedures: Committee on Scientific and Professional Ethics and Conduct. *American Psychologist, 29,* 703–710.
American Psychological Association. (1977). *Standards for providers of psychological services* (rev. ed.). Washington, DC: Author.
American Psychological Association. (1981a). *Ethical principles of psychologists.* Washington, DC: Author.
American Psychological Association. (1981b). Specialty guidelines for the delivery of services by counseling psychologists. *American Psychologist, 36,* 652–663.
Ethics Committee of the American Psychological Association. (1985). Rules and procedures. *American Psychologist, 40,* 685–694.
Jacobs, O. F. (1976). Standards for psychologists. In H. Dorken & Associates (Eds.), *The professional psychologist today: New developments in law, health insurance and health practice* (pp. 19–32). San Francisco: Jossey Bass.
Mills, D. H. (1984). Ethics education and adjudication within psychology. *American Psychologist, 39,* 669–695.
Van Hoose, W. H., & Kottler, J. A. (1985). *Ethical and legal issues in counseling.* San Francisco: Jossey Bass.
Welfel, E. R., & Lipsitz, N. E. (1984). The ethical behavior of professional psychologists: A critical analysis of the research. *The Counseling Psychologist, 12,* 31–42.

Chapter Two
Values in Ethical Counseling

Garth Sorenson and Lisa V. Kassoy[*]

For several decades it has been fashionable to speak of "values-free" counseling. Counselors should not "impose their values on clients," the slogan goes, the implication being that in matters of ethics and values any person's opinion is as good as the next. Furthermore, efforts to employ moral rules in counseling would automatically result in such prima facie evils as emotional repression and overt social control. Recently, however, there has been growing recognition that counseling inevitably involves the values of both counselor and client; that, intentionally or not, counselors act as moral agents; and that those counselors who posit values-free counseling apparently fail to understand the meaning of morality and thus run the risk that their actions will have immoral consequences.

This chapter proceeds from the premise that many counselors have been inadequately trained in moral philosophy. Yet it is not as simple as just recognizing that one's value orientations affect one's actions. Counselors also need an explicit set of moral guidelines—"maxims," to use Polanyi's (1964) word—to guide their everyday work. The rules must be of such a nature that they will withstand public inspection, including the scrutiny of those who are knowledgeable in ethics and related fields. The guidelines must be considerably more comprehensive than the rules that usually constitute statements of professional ethics, e.g., American Psychological Association ethical standards. And certainly they must take us beyond mere "values clarification."

---

[*]University of California at Los Angeles, School of Education.

Clearly, given the nature of morality, no one can expect to put together an absolute, permanent, unassailable set of moral guidelines. But by focusing on what people of goodwill can agree on rather than concentrating on the points of disagreement, it should be possible to develop a preliminary set of guidelines that will have value as a framework for further discussion and a reference in counseling practice. With sufficient study and revision, these guidelines could perhaps serve as a standard of moral competence for the profession as a whole.

In this chapter we will discuss some issues regarding values that we believe to be fundamental to the development of a moral/ethical framework for counselors. First, we will argue that counselors are moral agents whether they intend to be or not, illustrating with actual counseling cases how values and issues of moral philosophy play a role in ethical counseling. Then we will review some propositions drawn from moral philosophy that seem to us useful in their implications for the counselor's social role. Finally, we will state and attempt to defend our position concerning the role of values in counseling and the need for a set of ethical guidelines for counseling.

ETHICAL ISSUES CONFRONTING COUNSELORS

Many (perhaps most) of the problems that people bring to counselors are moral as well as psychological. Should I divorce my wife? Evade the draft? Have an abortion? Give up college for myself and get a job to help put my brother, husband, or boyfriend through school? Commit suicide? Put my to-be-born baby up for adoption? Tell the Student Store that one of my acquaintances is systematically stealing books? Inform the police that someone I know is pushing drugs? Tell a professor that one of her assistants is faking research data or that one of the students had someone else write her term paper? These are all questions that counselors have been asked by counselees at one time or another, and it would be easy to list a great many more like them. Whether or not one thinks of oneself as a moralist, to deal with such questions—or to decide not to deal with them—requires that one take a moral position and apply moral rules, even though there is disagreement among moral philosophers as to what those moral rules should be and how they should be derived.

Occasionally, counselors find themselves faced with moral problems brought by someone other than a client. Sometimes a superordinate will direct a counselor to act in ways that the counselor considers unethical, e.g., a principal will tell the counselor that his or her job is to administer punishment to students who violate school regulations, or ask him or her for information that the counselor considers confidential. The fact that a superordinate requires a counselor to do something and thereby bears responsibility for the counselor's actions does not obviate the fact that these are moral issues for which the counselor too carries responsibility.

The point at which counselors most need moral rules is in determining what the treatment goals should be in a particular case— or even whether the counselor should get involved at all. Frequently, counselors appear to be altogether unaware that in the decision to take particular clinical actions, or in the decision not to take such actions, there has been an implicit ethical choice. Perhaps a few examples will help illustrate this point:

Case 1. During the early 1970s, a graduate student told the members of a class of the following moral dilemma. Some months earlier, while working as a counselor in a junior high school, he learned from two of the junior high school boys that a third boy had told them and several others that he was going to give a girl a mixture of drugs that included strychnine. Because it sounded dangerous to them and because they believed he might actually do what he said he was going to do, the two thought they should tell someone. The counselor was troubled by their report, and yet quite undecided about what he should do. Would an intelligent 13-year-old really do such a thing? Were the two informers trying to get the other boy into trouble to settle an old score? Was it really counseling business—should a counselor suddenly assume the role of policeman? Were the boys playing a practical joke on him, and would other faculty members laugh at his gullibility if he reported it? Would he lose credibility with the other students of the school if he "violated confidentiality"? The whole thing seemed so incredible and so complex that he decided to "sleep on it" over night. The upshot was that the boy did give the girl some poisonous concoction of drugs. By the time a physician got to the girl, it was too late to save her. The counselor told his fellow graduate students that he was still haunted by the incident and by the question of whether he should have taken some action, or whether he was correct, because he was a counselor, in letting matters take their course.

The other students in the class, mainly teachers and counselors, tried to reassure him. They said it would not have been appropriate for him to intervene; that he'd done the right thing by not turning "stool pigeon"; that he'd had bad luck; that this kind of thing could happen to anyone; that, on the other hand, it was unique—they'd never heard of a case exactly like this before and never expected to hear of one like it again; that everyone has 20–20 hindsight but only rarely the foresight to deal with such a case. But at the end of the discussion, the counselor said that he was still troubled.

The instructor was troubled too, and not just by the tragedy. During those years most professional counselors, at least in public, appeared to assume a strong "nondirective" stance in which they focused almost exclusively on a client's feelings and often rejected what would normally be regarded as intelligent actions. The counselor telling the story had faced a rare if not unique situation, had acted on the basis of his information and his training, and had guessed wrong about the significance of information that he did not entirely trust. As Kaplan (1963) notes, "Morality is rarely a matter simply of applying an unquestioned principle to a case that indubitably falls under its scope. The moral problem is to weigh the conflicting principles and to act on a balance of probabilities on behalf of the preponderant values" (p. 91). But the instructor felt that the glib reassurance of the counselor candidates and counselors in the class, and his own indecision about the case, were indicators that something very important was lacking in the professional curriculum.

Case 2. The following incident occurred at a junior high school. During the course of a visit, a consultant spent some hours talking with groups of students about their perceptions of themselves, the counseling office, the school, and related matters. He asked a group of ninth-graders what a student had to do to be popular in the school. There was a lively and serious discussion during which students stated their opinions and disagreements freely. For the most part they were thoughtful, good-humored, and polite to one another. They agreed that far and away the most effective way of becoming popular with both boys and girls was to learn how to make other students laugh. Unfortunately, that was a very difficult skill to acquire, they said, and only a few had mastered the art. The second most effective means of acquiring popularity was to demonstrate skill in the "chop sessions." The chop session was a verbal contest in which two or three students would exchange insults. Apparently a participant won admiration from the onlookers in two ways. One was to be able to deliver a series of witty hurtful remarks, to engage in biting repartee. The other was to demonstrate self-control—to absorb insults without crying or "blowing one's cool." The student who was able to make the other cry while maintaining his or her own composure gained status. The students described a third way of gaining popularity, not really all that effective but the only thing some kids could do, that is, to become a good fighter. Chicanos often resorted to fighting because they felt that they didn't have the verbal facility to make others laugh nor the temperament to enjoy the chop sessions, and so about all they could do to gain prestige was to fight. In fact, a girl fight was scheduled that afternoon, halfway between the school and the barrio, at about four o'clock. They let the consultant know it would be an embarrassment if he showed up because the faculty in that school preferred not to know about such matters. They went on to say that there were a few students, who couldn't make others laugh and weren't good in the chop sessions or fighting, who resorted to grade-getting. But so far as anyone in the room of mainly upper-middle-class kids could recall, no one in that school had ever achieved popularity by getting good grades.

During the course of the discussion, there was one student whom the girls, in particular, ganged up on. They took turns making pointed remarks about his smoking on campus, his having been suspended from the football team for missing practice sessions, and his other violations of school rules. Their tone and manner, while superficially friendly, were sharp, superior, and smug. And they were persistent, would not let up. There were moments when it appeared that their victim, although the largest person in the room, was about to break into tears. It was hard to understand why he did not request permission to leave the group and go back to his class. Later the consultant asked the counselor about him.

"He is the brightest student in the school," she said, "and I am afraid we are going to lose him. I spend a lot of time trying to keep him in school. But his classmates are driving him out."

The consultant asked her if she ought to intervene more directly in the affair—for example, if she'd thought of saying something to the other students about it, whether she might discuss the matter with two or three of those bright, pretty, cruel girls who seemed to be the ringleaders. The counselor said rather stiffly that she did not think that intervening would be appropriate nor consistent with the counselor's role. None of the students had requested such an intervention. The conversation turned to other matters.

Case 3. In an in-service training class in which a number of junior high school counselors were enrolled, the consultant was asking about the most troublesome problems the counselors encountered on their jobs. One of the men said that he'd been trying to do career planning with some eighth- and ninth-grade boys. He'd asked them what occupations they were interested in, and most of them listed pimp as their first choice. At first he thought they were kidding him, but he soon discovered they were quite serious. They said there was more money to be made in pimping than in any other occupation that was open to black men, and with less effort. They knew because they knew pimps, would see them on the streets where they lived, driving Cadillacs, flashing thick rolls of bills, wearing expensive clothes and diamond rings. And there were side benefits—girls.

As a counselor, what should he do, he wondered. Help the boys get into the "occupation of their choice"? Try to transfer to another school? Give up counseling? All that the other counselors, his fellow students in the class, could agree on was that as a counselor he should not impose his values.

In all three of these situations, potential counselees were engaging in behavior that was likely to be damaging to other persons, but again and again the argument was made that cases such as these are not within the scope of the counselors' responsibility. What are some of the ethical issues involved?

AVOIDING THE MORALIST'S ROLE

When we discuss these three cases with counseling students, we present them as merely extreme examples of some rather common problems. Reactions usually vary, but many students express a lack of interest in the anecdotes because they are not the kinds of problems with which counselors should be concerned. We had expected a strong response from the women's liberation contingent to the junior high school counselor's problem, on the grounds that pimping is an exploitive occupation. But some of the women maintained serenely that since it is not a counselor's job to impose values, they didn't believe the counselor should do anything beyond "values clarification." A few were derisive and suggested that only a very naive person would find pimping an objectionable occupation.

There are several obvious reasons why many counselors want to avoid the role of moralist. Most obvious perhaps is the fact that the term "moralist," in common usage, connotes a prudish, narrow, rigid, self-righteous, tedious, nagging sort of person who has little or no understanding of the views and feelings of others and who is basically too sour and intolerant ever to counsel anyone. Still, granted that self-righteous and tedious moralizing is likely to be counterproductive in counseling, surely not all ethical counseling need take that form.

We have a hunch that a second reason some counselors insist that counselors should not be moral/ethical agents is that they equate ethics and religion and believe that morals are purely within the domain of the rabbi, minister, or priest. Some people, because they have discarded or avoided religion, have also discarded a conscious concern for ethics, believing it to be merely another trapping of religion. The social behavior of most of this group may often conform to high moral standards, and yet they scoff at discussions of moral problems. Granting the important historical and continuing role of the churches in teaching moral codes, our own position is that morality doesn't necessarily have anything to do with religion. Many of the individuals who have contributed to ethical thought (see Chapter 3) are not or were not themselves religious in any sectarian sense.

A third reason some counselors are uninterested in an explicit moral philosophy derives from their preoccupation with counseling techniques and from their consequent lack of attention to counseling outcomes. For example, Carl Rogers and his disciples have said that counselors should not be judgmental, should not give advice, and should have unconditional regard for their clients. Rogers's early "nondirective" principles are still highly regarded by many counselors, who apparently have accepted them as tenets and thus never question a client's values, perceptions, or goals, trusting that the client's wisdom will be released through the instrumentality of a therapeutic relationship. Most counselors who call themselves "humanistic" are vehement in their insistence on avoiding any interventions that might be seen as encroachment on a client's freedom and responsibility for making his own choices.

Other counselors focus single-mindedly on the goals of the individual client without apparent concern about the impact of the client's behavior on the others in his life. Wolpe, for example, quoted by Patterson (1986) on the topic of treating male sexual inadequacy, says that if the husband cannot obtain the cooperation of his wife in the treatment process, the therapist should see her in order to obtain it. If the wife still will not cooperate, "it is usually appropriate to encourage the husband to seek out another woman who may be more responsive to him" (p. 118). From this perspective, the restoration of the husband's potency may improve the marriage, but even if it does not, the man is better off. Women graduate students, on reading the bit about "encouraging the husband to seek out another woman," objected to both the moral and psychological implications of this approach to counseling.

But perhaps the most important reason that counselors avoid the role of moral agent has to do with a misconception relating to moral relativism. From earliest time, moral philosophers have reflected on two kinds of questions that concern us here (Fineberg, 1969). One is the question of ultimate purposes. For example, what are the goods most worth having? What sort of person is most worth being? The second is the question of how we are to know, or who is to say? Counselors who know cultural anthropology often believe "it is a matter of fact that moral rules are invented by peoples, and that almost any practice that is prohibited in one culture will be approved in another" (Benedict, 1934). An apparently increasing number of people during recent decades have assumed that if "the authorities" cannot agree on the grounds for moral truths, then moral rules may perhaps be anthropologically interesting but must not be very important, and all moral positions must have equal claim to validity (Perry, 1968; Chapter 4, this volume).

But moral principles are not purely subjective. As Kaplan (1963), Warnock (1971), and other philosophers have pointed out, moral principles can be and are tested against logic and experience. Furthermore, as Kaplan observed, agreement on the source of moral rules is not necessary for moral consensus: "Just as differences in epistemology do not prevent acceptance of the same body of scientific truths, [so the] same public morality can be grounded in a belief in God, man, or nature" (p. 91).

The nihilistic ethical position appears, at least to the amateur in philosophy, to have gathered strength from the fact that for some decades moral philosophers chose to limit moral philosophy to the study of the language of morals (Hare, 1964). Phillipa Foot (1967), among others, has expressed the opinion that 25 years of studying the language of ethics has turned out to be of relatively little benefit to moral philosophy. What counselors have needed and still need is help in figuring out how to apply moral rules to such common daily problems as marital disputes and child-rearing conflicts. Fortunately, moral philosophers now have begun again to give attention to such issues (see, for example, Barnes, 1978; Thalberg & Fellow, 1979; & Wilson, 1978).

SOME INTERPRETATIONS
FROM MORAL PHILOSOPHY

Our purposes are not to present a summation of the various conflict-ing views of moral philosophers but rather to draw on this body of thought for certain propositions about "values" that we believe most people in Western society will endorse and that, we shall try to show, have relevance for counseling. One source of ideas lies in an ex-amination of the social sources of morality and another in the relationship between moral and legal roles. A review of these con-cepts makes it clear that moral judgment is an intellectual enter-prise that requires both knowledge and reasoning skills.

Social Sources of Morality and Values

Morality may be seen as a system of practical rules based on the collective wisdom of mankind concerning the consequences of par-ticular actions (Baier, 1965). Moral codes are not instinctual but must be learned. That is not to reject Waddington's (1967) observa-tion that the processes of evolution have resulted in an "ethical animal" and that moral behavior has survival value. Many philosophers, e.g., Protagoras, Hobbes, Hume, Warnock, Rawls (see Mackie, 1977), and others, e.g., Lippmann (1956), have observed that human beings need rules for living together harmoniously and cooperatively within a society.

Downie (1971) and Warnock (1971) have listed a number of observations about people and their environment that provide a basis for thinking about the evolution of moral systems: human beings become "human" only in societies. They lack individual self-sufficiency, having needs that cannot be met by each alone. Because of their limitations in intelligence, knowledge, skills, and un-derstanding, their achievements—and survival—often depend on cooperation. Cooperation is uncertain, for people also have "limited benevolence and confined generosity" (Downie, 1971). Experience plays an important role in determining the social organization that people will accept. In some cultures, scarcity has given rise to the concept of personal property and to an entire network of generally accepted rules about its acquisition and exchange. Although mutually dependent, people are still motivated by self-interest and, given the many environmental as well as individual limitations, often are pitted against one another in situations where interests conflict. As Baier (1965) argues, the concept of morality exists because people live in societies, have continuing interactions with one another, and cannot avoid having conflicts from time to time (see Rest in Chapter 4, this volume).

Values and the Law

Roughly speaking, values are the moral rules that are something like the laws of the land. Our written laws can be regarded as one subset of moral rules. Even though the laws and rules of different communities may be somewhat different from one another, every community needs moral rules in order to survive, and the rules need to be enforced. People, including counselors, need to know what the rules are and try to obey them. Complying is admittedly complicated, however, because we have a great many laws and moral rules, they are often inconsistent with one another, and they gradually change over time.

In order to preserve society and to live effectively within it, individuals must learn to exercise rational choice. Insofar as an individual is rational and able to choose, he or she is capable of moral agency. And since individuals derive benefits from living within a society, each is morally obligated to live by its rules (Wilson, 1978). Indeed, except for the legally incompetent, the role of social agent is unavoidable. Downie (1971) points out that even persons who decide they need not consider any moral claims on themselves, those who just do not bother to do so, and those who act immorally continue to be moral agents. One cannot by one's choice abdicate the role of moral agent, for the decision to abdicate is itself a moral position.

Moral Judgment, Values, Knowledge, and Reasoning

Morality works by providing social direction and control to the members of a society in making practical judgments as to what they should and should not do, and it gives them practical reasons for doing what they should do (Baier, 1965). Moral judgments are arrived at by surveying the facts of the situation and applying to them "rules of reason", or the society's "consideration-making beliefs." Polanyi (1964) prefers the term "maxim" to name the kinds of values or moral rules we are talking about here. One such rule might be that when evaluating means and ends, ends are to be given more value than means. Counselors often seem to be guilty of violating this rule when they avoid discussing short-term and long-term outcomes of their own and their clients' behaviors.

People presumably use their moral rules to establish criteria for making comparisons and rankings among alternative actions, to guide them in considering consequences, and to determine, more or less consciously, which course of action a "reasonable" individual would choose. The process of moral judgment requires knowledge of the common rules of behavior such as laws, conventions, and manners and also some ability to reason. Both the knowledge of rules and the reasoning skills must be acquired, and it is probably true that, in virtually all societies, the elders feel morally obligated to teach these to younger generations.

THE ROLE OF VALUES IN COUNSELING

Counselors operate within the same system of moral obligation and responsibility as do all other members of the society. They are no more able to function in a values-free fashion than any other individual, and in fact, because of the nature of the duties and obligations inherent in their role, they may be said to have a special and greater responsibility as moral agents than most others have. For as Williamson (1958) suggested several decades ago, the job of the counselor is to teach clients how to think rationally about their personal problems and how to arrive at decisions that are morally sound and not merely satisfying. While guiding clients in the process of analyzing their capabilities, aptitudes, interests, motivations, resources, limitations, and so on, in order to make plans that are likely to provide long-range satisfactions, the counselor should help them weigh the potential effects of the alternatives they contemplate on the "significant others" in their lives—their parents, spouses, children (see "Stage of Empathy," Chapter 4, this volume).

Whether consciously and deliberately or covertly and unintentionally, counselors will indeed influence the values and, consequently, the behavior of their clients. And we predict that, as social learning theories—particularly Bandura's (1977) version—come to play a more prominent role in counseling psychology, counselors will gradually become more sensitive to and gain a better understanding of the role they play as models to be imitated by clients.

Intentionally or not, counselors have always acted as moral pedagogues, and this role is very subtle and very complex. Along with others in the mental health professions, counselors help to define a conception of "optimal human functioning" and to establish criteria for describing the "good life" and the "mentally healthy" individual; and they set counseling objectives consistent with their definitions. All of these operations involve value judgments. In the very act of selecting or accepting "cases," counselors employ rules and guidelines based on value judgments about what constitutes less than optimal functioning and who will profit most from treatment. The counselor's values will certainly influence the choice of clients with whom to work, the objectives of counseling, and the interventions used (Williamson, 1958). The counselor's values, the values of "the authority," also are the values that the cooperative client will learn to know as being true.

Indeed many believe that counselors and psychotherapists have become "secular priests." Jerome Frank (1976) gives an explanation of how they achieved this status. Psychotherapies, he says, flourish in times of social change, when the traditional, generally accepted values and institutions become discredited. When the means for transmitting mankind's accumulated wisdom weaken, as with the weakening of family and church, the traditional institutions lose power to unite the members of society and to provide a view of the world that gives meaning to life. Many "demoralized" people—demoralized because they feel they have lost the power to control and improve their lives—will turn to psychology to fill the void left by the attrition of traditional and religiously sanctioned values.

Most of the counselors whom we know would probably not happily see themselves in the role of secular priest. They tend to define their own professional roles much more narrowly. Some appear to see themselves as more like technicians than professionals.

On one hand, it can be considered avoiding appropriate role responsibilities when counselors deny their ethical responsibilities in counseling; still, counselors cannot be too eager to grasp the role of moral authority without making explicit how their values and moral criteria will be used to define standards of mental health, therapeutic objectives, appropriate treatment interventions, and means of assessing and controlling for unwanted treatment outcomes. Counselors will have to think through their own ethical assumptions and the values underlying their choices and review the relationships between means and end states. Counselors should guard against becoming too process-oriented and too fad-hungry to be willing to give time and effort to specifying and measuring the role of values in their counseling.

In addition, counselors must consider the assumptions underlying the policies of both the agencies in which they work and the institutions that support them, insofar as these assumptions concern the nature of human behavior, social values, and the role and purpose of counseling. Such assumptions can be disguised or undeclared, yet they will influence the objectives toward which the counselor's professional efforts are directed. For example, consequences of the sexual counseling policies that encourage husbands to "seek out another woman" may be more divorces, more one-parent homes, and a shift in the value and meaning of loyalty and fidelity in the society at large. We don't have data on this particular topic, but would most counselors feel that such possible "side effects" were acceptable? Would the counseling profession's constituency find it so?

The values of counselors and the values of agencies may conflict, and counselors will need to make ethical decisions when confronting these dilemmas. The issues involve individual versus collective goods, humanitarian versus institutional demands and obligations, and so on. Some counselors need to confront the potential conflicts of professional codes of ethics and policies of organizations that reflect racism, sexism, or social injustice. Certainly counselors cannot deal with client behavior generated by the social system without either strengthening or altering that system in some way. There are signs that the courts are beginning to require counselors to conform to prescribed ethical guidelines about the "sanctity of life" and prohibitions about murder in their practice. It would seem preferable for such guidelines to be the product of the profession's own reflection.

SUMMARY

If counseling is to contribute to the well-being of both clients and the society of which they are a part, the complex and consequential process of specifying the counselor's values, of examining community and agency values, and of reconciling any differences among them cannot be merely intuitive. It is for this reason, ultimately, that counselors urgently need to develop guidelines regarding the role of values in ethical counseling. These guidelines should comprise not only the maxims or statements of values needed by counselors in their daily work but also those philosophical beliefs that can constitute the counselors' curricula as "values" agents, to be taught to and used by clients for coping with problems of everyday life.

REFERENCES

Baier, K. (1965). *The moral point of view.* New York: Random House.

Bandura, A. (1977). Self-efficacy: Toward a unifying theory of behavioral change. *Psychological Review, 84,* 191–215.

Barnes, H. E. (1978). *An existentialist ethics.* Chicago: University of Chicago Press.

Benedict, R. (1934). *Patterns of culture.* Boston: Houghton Mifflin.

Downie, R. S. (1971). *Roles and values.* London: Methuen.

Fineberg, J. (Ed.). (1969). *Moral concepts.* New York: Oxford University Press.

Foot, P. (Ed.). (1967). *Theories of ethics.* New York: Oxford University Press.

Frank, J. D. (1976). *Persuasion and healing* (2nd ed.). New York: Schocken Books.

Hare, R. M. (1964). *The language of morals.* New York: Oxford University Press.

Kaplan, A. (1963). *American ethics and public policy.* New York: Oxford University Press.

Lippmann, W. (1956). *The public philosophy.* New York: New American Library (Mentor).

Mackie, J. L. (1977). *Ethics.* New York: Penguin.

Patterson, C. H. (1986). *Theories of counseling and psychotherapy* (4th ed.). New York: Harper and Row.

Perry, W. (1968). *Forms of intellectual and ethical development in the college years: A scheme.* New York: Holt, Rinehart and Winston.

Polanyi, M. (1964). *Personal knowledge.* New York: Harper (Torchbooks).

Waddington, C. H. (1967). *The ethical animal.* Chicago: University of Chicago Press (Phoenix).

Warnock, G. J. (1971). *The object of morality.* London: Methuen.

Williamson, E. G. (1958). Value orientation in counseling. *Personnel and Guidance Journal, 36,* 519–528.

Wilson, J. R. S. (1978). In one another's power. *Ethics, 88,* 299–316.

Chapter Three
Philosophical Basis of Professional Ethics

MORAL STANDARDS

This chapter discusses various proposals regarding moral standards. When making these proposals, philosophers have generally emphasized either duty or purpose. Those who emphasize duty argue that men and women have a duty to perform certain actions whether they can see any immediate good resulting from them or not. Using a formal moral criterion, these theories argue that some actions are intrinsically right or wrong irrespective of their consequences. Formal criteria of rightness for making moral judgments have been derived from (a) the authority of God, (b) an individual's conscience, and/or (c) principles such as Immanuel Kant's categorical imperative.

Another group of philosophers who discuss universal moral standards emphasize the importance of purpose and argue that no behavior is in itself inherently right or wrong. People's actions are judged only in reference to their purposes and the consequences of their actions. These philosophers have proposed that the criteria for the "good life" may include such consequences as pleasure, self-realization, and fulfillment of interest.

In contrast to both of these groups are those philosophers who criticize the whole idea of fixed moral standards. For them, the ultimate moral values of men and women do and should change. Every moral situation is in itself a unique event, and that fact alone should lead one to conclude that intelligence should be the major factor in morality. The practical meaning of any situation is not self-evident and has to be discovered through intellectual inquiry. The individual's task is to determine a right course of action and a right good in a moral situation that involves conflicting desires and apparent alternative goods. The argument is that a person's actions should be judged less by absolute moral standards than by the direction in which the person is moving in his or her search for the ethical answers.

The study of ethics is the study of the "individual good" and is particularly important to psychologists and counselors because they make decisions that often involve moral judgments about what is desirable, good, and right for themselves, for their clients, and for the profession. When professionals begin to think about such moral judgments, they are engaging in ethical inquiry and analyzing the role of "shoulds" in ethical counseling. Ethical counseling ultimately involves evaluating both counselor and client behaviors by reference to values, ideals, principles, and norms.

ETHICS OF ACTING AND JUDGING

An important distinction made by philosophers concerns the difference between the ethical problems of the moral agent (the ethics of acting) and the ethical problems of the moral judge (the ethics of judging). The professional clinician has ethical responsibilities related to his or her behavior in particular situations, as well as ethical responsibilities related to his or her judgments regarding the behavior of other professionals. Thus, a profession has a twofold teaching mission in the area of ethics: (a) to increase the quality of ethical reasoning and acting of individual members and (b) to increase the quality of ethical reasoning in the professional monitoring responsibilities of individual members and professional organizations. This distinction between the ethics of the actor and the ethics of the judge reflects two major issues in ethical counseling: (a) what are the criteria to be used by counselors and counseling psychologists to guide their professional actions and (b) what are the criteria to be used for professional monitoring and making judgments about the actions of individual professionals. For instance, in the ethics of acting, the professional person is considering philosophical criteria to be used when making inferences and hypotheses regarding the possible ethical implications of his or her own actions. In the ethics of judging, the professional person is making inferences regarding the quality of the ethical judgments of another professional person. Of necessity the judge is faced with making ethical inferences involving a degree of second-guessing.

In our discussion of moral standards and the relevance of the ensuing arguments for defining the nature of right and wrong in ethical counseling, please keep in mind that we need to consider both the ethics of acting and the ethics of judging. However, in the case of ethics of judging, remember that we are dealing with two issues: the accuracy of the judges' inferences about the ethical criteria used by an individual counselor and the ethical criteria to be used by the judges in their evaluation of the ethical actions of another person. For professionals to be ethical judges or monitors of other professionals' ethical responsibilities they must be capable of examining their own thinking about the thinking and acting of others.

PHILOSOPHICAL STANDARDS AND PROFESSIONAL ETHICS

In all areas of professional life, the counselor is called on to make ethical judgments concerning his or her rights and obligations, others' rights and obligations, and judgments about values to be used in resolving any conflicts of role expectations. In such situations, assumptions are made regarding the nature of ideal conditions or states, and perceptions of present conditions are compared to those ideal conditions. Philosophers over the ages have debated about the logical arguments to support various statements regarding these "ethical ideal states." Ethical principles based on models of ideal states will guide a counselor in choosing appropriate actions in a wide variety of situations involving moral dilemmas. These principles should be universal in their scope and contain universal prescriptions. Ethical principles are *fundamental* if they identify general moral obligations that are relevant or applicable to many actual situations. Fundamental ethical principles will state the conditions that need to be fulfilled for there to be a moral obligation or duty involved. The conditions are then usually expressed in relation to a particular conception of the nature of "the good life" or an ethical ideal state. Steinmeyer, Newell, and Garcia (1984) describe secondary moral principles as being situationally specific and dealing with specific classes of actions that should be taken in specific cases. For example, such principles might include truth, privacy, promise-keeping, and the sanctity of life.

Fundamental Ethical Principles: God's Will

One major criterion for judging whether an action is ethical or not has been in terms of the will of God. Simply stated, God's will determines what is good and bad. However, this statement begs the perplexing question, how do we know the will of God? William Paley, a popular moralist of the 18th century, said the answer to this question was to be found in scriptural revelation and the "light of nature" (Castell, 1943). The former is a fairly well understood source of moral guidance; however, the latter criterion of morality—the "light of nature"—is less clearly defined. To ascertain the will of God when there is no express statement in scripture one must inquire into the tendency of an action to promote or diminish the general happiness. The assumption is that God intended humans to be happy. If you accept the position that the will of God determines what is right and wrong, then you would determine the will of God by reading scripture and following the general rule that good acts promote "general happiness."

Obedience. Another viewpoint about God and ethics was explored by the 19th-century theologian Bruner (1961), who argued that an act is right only if it is done in obedience to the direct personal command of God. In specific situations God issues commands to people. Obedient behavior defines the nature of what is good in these situations. Good actions are to be based on faith. The argument is that the nature of what is good cannot be determined on the basis of principles, whether they are religious or hedonistic. Using principles to define what is good is legalistic and on that basis should be rejected. The use of principles in ethical decision-making assumes that those principles allow one to predetermine what is right and what is wrong. Consequently, it follows that ethical principles cannot be used to determine what we ought to do in any specific situation. Only faith can guide our actions. The argument is that only believers can fully understand the Christian conception of the good. The good grows from the fact that man receives and accepts his life as a gift from God. The good is simply what God wills that we should do! God's will is often expressed by His sanctions, rewards, and punishments. The most important point is that we obey God because He commands it. The primary concern is to do God's will.

Somewhat surprisingly, an important aspect in following the will of God is to promote self-interest. An individual cannot do good acts unless such acts have significance for him. However, self-interest should always be rooted in the will of God.

Our Rational Nature. A very important group of philosophers who argued that the authority of God is the major criterion for making ethical decisions are the Scholastics and neo-Scholastics (Bourke, 1951). This group makes a distinction between moral good and evil on the basis of the very nature of human existence. Moreover, the basic ideas of good and evil, just and unjust, lawful and unlawful are the same at all times and among all people.

A morally good act is one that helps us to know and love God and in so doing contributes to the development of our rational nature. Any object of a morally good act can be considered morally good. On the other hand, moral evil is in opposition to our rational nature. For example, we condemn drunkenness and wild living because they degrade and disgrace us. From this perspective the overriding criterion for ethical decisions is the *natural law*. God has given to each of us a predisposition to know and will. Our rational nature exists because God implanted a natural law in each person that is rational and free and inclines us toward the real good, which is apprehended by our intellect. A person's moral obligations are based first on human nature and second on the wisdom of God who created that nature.

Commands of Conscience. Francis Wayland (1961) argued that conscience is God-given, and it provides the same moral commands to all men and women. Conscience is the faculty by which we discern the moral quality of actions, and our conscience also makes us capable of responding appropriately to these dictates. Our conscience is a distinctive human faculty, and it allows us to perceive the moral qualities in our experiences. The moral qualities of a person's actions are a reflection of his or her intentions. For example, it can never be considered right to respond intentionally to kindness by injuring someone. The point is that no person or class of persons can violate any moral precept without a feeling of guilt or a sense that they deserve punishment. Still, these "conscience" philosophers would allow for a defective or imperfect conscience. Although our conscience teaches us to recognize our moral obligations, human beings can still choose to obey or disobey their consciences. However, if we choose to disobey our consciences, we will be conscious of feelings of self-degradation.

The conscience philosophers tend to view human beings as composed of impulsive and restraining faculties. The impulsive faculties include our passions and appetites for activities that result in immediate satisfaction. Our self-interest and/or self-love also impels us to seek experiences that promote pleasure, passions, and self-interest. Conscience is the faculty that restrains our appetites so that we will refrain from injuring ourselves or others and will restrict our pursuit of happiness so as not to interfere with the happiness of others. Individual happiness as well as society as a whole is best served under conditions where conscience is supreme.

Philosophers differ about the origins of conscience. Some contend that conscience is God-given and universal, whereas others think conscience is a product of social learning and for that reason individuals have different consciences. The latter group point out that conscientious differences exist among people with similar heritages and environments, and that is the best reason that conscience cannot be used as a universal moral standard.

Fundamental Ethical Principles: The Authority of Duty

Rational Morality. Immanuel Kant, writing in the Age of Reason (1724–1804), provides a thought-provoking discussion of ethics (Castell, 1943; Kant, 1961). Of his many contributions, one of the most important is the concept of a rational morality as opposed to a theological morality. He argues that any idea that is true, is true categorically, true without any reference to why it is true. Rational morality is a fact to be recognized. It is a priori in character and binding on all rational beings.

For Kant, there are both principles of morality and motives or incentives to morality. An action is immoral whose principle cancels itself when it is made a universal rule. If an action is to be considered good in itself, the imperative for the act is categorical. To paraphrase Kant, we should act only on those principles that we would be willing to have as *universal* laws. When we act out of respect for this principle, we are following our duty.

Moral acts are done because duty requires them and not simply because they are in accord with what duty requires. To be moral we should only do things because they are absolutely right in themselves; a good will leads one to do what ought to be done.

Kant has defined the ultimate moral principle as "the categorical imperative." This standard of morality is a motivation for performing right actions simply because they are right. All imperatives are expressed by the word *ought* and indicate the relation of an "objective law of reason" to the "subjective imperfection of the individual's will."

Kant gives an example of how to apply his views to an actual case: A man wishes to commit suicide. He asks whether the principle underlying this action could become a universal law of nature. This principle might be stated as follows: Based on self-love as a principle I plan to shorten my life because living any longer is likely to bring me more unhappiness than satisfaction. The question is, can this principle based on self-love become a universal law of nature? Kant argues against it. A system of nature or life cannot have a universal law to destroy life using as a reason the very feelings of self-love that are supposed to be the basis for improving life. Such a principle would contradict itself and therefore could not exist as a system of nature. For that reason, the principle used to justify the person's suicide cannot possibly exist as a universal law of nature and thus is immoral.

Another reason for Kant's position on suicide is implied in the practical imperative, which states that one should act so as to treat humanity, including oneself, in every case as an *end* itself and never as a *means* to an end.

Fundamental Ethical Principles: Virtues and Vices

Realistic ethics is based on the laws of nature, happiness or well-being, and virtue (Aristotle, 1961a, 1961b). These natural laws are a part of the very nature of human beings and are objective and universal. Happiness or well-being is the goal of our human nature, and it is the goal of all moral effort. Happiness includes those human activities that are in accord with virtues and good habits. Self-realization is humanity's highest good and can be found in activities that involve exercise of the virtue of contemplative reasoning and in traits such as courage, friendship, and justice.

Aristotle's major ethical work, the *Nicomachean Ethics*, outlines the bases for realistic ethics (Aristotle, 1961b). First of all, it makes a distinction between intellectual excellence and moral excellence. The former is a consequence of instruction, whereas the latter is the result of habit or custom. The major assumption in realistic ethics is that virtue aims toward the midpoint or mean, and that is the reason that virtue is considered moderation.

Virtues are the aspects of your character that result from your choices. We become just people by doing just acts, temperate people by doing temperate acts, and brave people by doing brave acts. Accordingly, the kinds of habits we form in our youth make all the difference in our adult behavior. Human virtues are those aspects of character that make a person good and cause him or her to perform well. Simply stated, our virtues are those characteristics that result from choices based on moderation and motivated by rational and practical principles. Happiness is produced by those human activities that are in accord with our virtues. Any excesses or deficiencies in our behavior reflect vices, whereas moderation reflects virtues.

Vices fall short of or exceed what is right; virtues find and choose that which is moderate. However, it is not always easy to find the middle road. Anyone can get too angry. It is easy to give or spend too much money. But to behave moderately with each person, to the right extent, at the right time, with the right motive, and in the right way is seldom done. It is never easy. That is why goodness is rare, laudable, and noble.

Although the goal of human nature is happiness, that is not to be equated simply with amusement or relaxation. The virtuous life requires exertion, and thus very seldom will virtue involve amusements. The better of any two parts of our personality is the more serious and the contemplative. A life of reason is best and most pleasant because reason more than anything else is the distinctive part of our human character.

The study of ethics should be the study of virtues or values and subsequent actions based on them. Real moral virtues always involve choice, rational principles, and thought or reflection. A person can act justly or unjustly only when the person does so voluntarily, and if a person ever acts in ignorance or under compulsion, his or her acts are to be considered involuntary. Based on this assumption regarding the voluntary nature of ethical acts, there are three possible ethical issues in social situations. *Mistakes* are injuries that result from ignorance, and the fault resides in the person. The person doesn't realize that his or her actions can result in injuries to other people. *Accidents* are injuries that are contrary to reasonable expectations. Although the outcomes are contrary to reasonable expectations, there is no reason to believe the individual's behavior reflected bad intentions. The fault lies outside of the person. *Injustices* are injuries based on knowledge and are the result of lack of deliberation. Injuries to others that result from anger or passion are considered acts of injustice, although the actors may not be considered unjust or wicked because the injuries are not due to their bad intentions. In those cases in which people choose, after reflection, to do unjust acts, they are acting like unjust and vicious people.

Fundamental Ethical Principles:
The Authority of Happiness and Pleasure

John Stuart Mill (1806–1873) argued that actions are right and good if they produce more happiness than would any other actions possible in the particular circumstances (Castell, 1943; Mill, 1961). Happiness is intended to promote pleasure and the absence of pain; unhappiness promotes pain and the depriving of pleasure. However, the standard for making judgments is not an individual's own greatest happiness or hedonism but the greatest amount of happiness for mankind.

Mill, like Aristotle, argues that morality is a matter of consequences. However, Mill claims that it is necessary always to calculate the consequences of "classes" of actions. We must look at individual actions as though multiplied and in large masses. For example, it could be argued that certain vicious and cruel people should be killed because the balance of consequences for this particular act would weigh greatly in favor of the consequences associated with killing them. However, the argument based on the philosophy of utilitarianism is that if people are free to kill all people they consider vicious because they are not worried about the consequences, no one's life would be safe!

Some forms of pleasure are to be considered more desirable and are more valuable than others. Mental pleasures are always superior to bodily pleasures because of their circumstantial advantages rather than their intrinsic nature. The ethical person will estimate both the quantity and the quality of pleasures. If one of two pleasures is by far preferred by those who are competently acquainted with both, even though it is associated with more discontent, and if those persons would not forgo the pleasure for any quantity of other pleasures, they are justified in describing the preferred pleasure as being superior in quality to the other pleasures. Based on this argument, if an individual is deciding between the quality of two pleasures and the relative pains associated with both, he or she would have to consider the feelings and judgments of experienced people (authorities).

The intelligent person requires more to be happy, is more capable of acute suffering, and is more accessible to such suffering at more points in time than the person of inferior intelligence would be. A highly intellectually endowed person (in contrast to the person who is less endowed) knows that any future happiness will always be imperfect. However, the intelligent person learns to bear the imperfections in life. He or she realizes that it is better to be a dissatisfied human being than a satisfied pig; better to be Socrates dissatisfied than a fool satisfied. If the fool has a different opinion than the wise man, it is because the fool has considered only one side of the issue whereas the wise man knows both sides.

Fundamental Ethical Principles: The Authority of Human Interests

For William James, the aim of morality should be to satisfy as many obligations as we can (Castell, 1943; James, 1961). Actions are judged good when they promote this ideal of meeting obligations and wrong when they interfere with its attainment.

The argument is that nothing is good or right except insofar as someone perceives it to be good or thinks it to be right. If one person's "ideal judgment" is better than another's, that superiority is a function of someone's perception or viewpoint. The terms *good* and *bad*, like the concept of obligations, have no absolute character independent of individual perceptions. For example, without a claim being made by some actual person, which is in turn perceived by another person, there can be no obligation. If we accept the argument that the bases of obligations are claims made by someone that are perceived as claims by another person, then how does the latter person determine what claims of others should take precedence? James concluded that one needs to assume that the claims of a living god must come first. In order to have a systematic unified moral truth, an individual must postulate the existence of a "Divine Thinker" even though his or her thoughts are not directly known to us. Our view of a Divine Thinker allows us to evaluate the ethics of our actions in situations involving conflicts of role expectations between ourselves and others.

The ethical world involves individuals who are making judgments about good and ill and who are making demands on one another. In this real world, whether God exists or not, the people living on earth are responsible for the ethical conditions. Thus, both the *religion of humanity* and *theism* must be considered in weighing the ethical implications of our actions.

An act is to be considered right in any situation if that act will make most people satisfied and the smaller number dissatisfied. An ideal will be right if the ideal condition involves the least cost to other peoples' ideals. Even people who want the world to be peaceful should realize that achieving their ideals cannot be done in ways that will negate the demands of others. In cases of conflicting demands, one should use the conventionally recognized "good" standard or the customs of the community to resolve the conflicts. However, people can break the norms or rules of society provided they are willing to stake their lives and characters on their actions. Social experiments that are deviant from the prevailing norms are to be judged only by actual findings, and the ethical person will wait on facts before making judgments about these experiments.

Since there are no absolute evils and there are nonmoral goods, the highest ethical life consists at all times in the breaking of arbitrary rules that have grown too narrow for the actual case or situation. But in those cases where the person chooses to break with the prevailing norms of society, he or she should always seek to act to bring about the very largest total universe of good that can be envisioned.

Fundamental Ethical Principles: No Fixed Moral Standard

John Dewey (1859–1952) argued for a pluralistic view involving many dynamic individualized goods and goals, and thus the ethical person needs principles, criteria, and laws to analyze individual, unique ethical situations (Clark, 1957; Dewey, 1961). The primary significance of ultimate moral principles is in their application to concrete situations; thus, the emphasis in morality should be on how ethical principles are intelligently applied to real situations, and not on the abstract universal principles themselves.

The practical meaning of the ethical issues in a situation is not self-evident but has to be discovered. Only through inquiry can a person determine the right course of action in that situation. The process of intellectual inquiry involves making observations, analyzing factors, clarifying what is obscure, identifying the salient and superficial parts, tracing the consequences of various actions, and considering decisions to be tentative until it can be determined whether the anticipated and actual consequences agree. Moral failures are the result of careless, perverse judgments (stupidity) in concrete situations.

Moral life does not necessarily need to involve the following of fixed rules or the pursuit of fixed goals. Instead, the moral person can detect ills that need to be remedied in specific cases and then formulate plans and methods for dealing with the ills. The problem of evil involves the practical problems of reducing, alleviating, and removing the "evils of life." Moral goods and ends exist only in a person's actions.

Values cannot be divided into those that are intrinsic or inherent and those that are instrumental or extrinsic. This distinction is often a superficial justification for making "ideal" goods more important than tangible goods. Somehow, when intrinsic goods are divorced from the problems of daily life, those problems are of lesser importance. The materialism and brutality in parts of the economic life may be due to the fact that some people consider economic goals to be merely instrumental and not of any ethical consequence. Instead, these activities should be viewed as having intrinsic value. Such a change in perception regarding the "morality of means" and the "morality of end states" could possibly result in massive improvements in the quality of our economic life.

In the process of inquiry, mistakes should not be considered unavoidable accidents about which to feel sorry, nor should they be seen as moral sins to be forgiven. Mistakes are lessons in the wrong use of intelligence, and they should provide directions to determine better courses of action in the future. Moral life then will become flexible, vital, and growing. Every situation that involves a moral action should be considered of equal importance to all other situations, and needs and deficiencies of any particular situation should define the moral goals for that situation. These goals should be considered to have intrinsic value, not merely instrumental value. In a given situation the ideal end state or "good" is equal in worth to the good or end state of other situations and merits intelligent attention.

The criteria for ethically evaluating behavior need to be dynamic and developmental. The ethical person's acts will always reflect growth, improvement, and progress. The bad person is simply the person who is beginning to deteriorate, to grow less good, whereas the good person is moving to become better. Development is the only moral end state. This end state, or goal, is not a fixed place but the active process of transforming the existing situation. Happiness is also a developmental, active process of moving to higher, more complex stages of reasoning.

CONCLUSION

This chapter has briefly summarized the views of a number of different philosophers about the nature of moral standards. These statements provide a sample of philosophical arguments about various ethical criteria, and they can be useful to the counseling psychologist who is trying to develop his or her own theory of morals and approach to ethical counseling. The content of counselors' philosophical beliefs regarding right and wrong provides the third major cognitive component in ethical counseling, along with their knowledge of professional codes and their general beliefs about values.

In a very practical way, counselors' knowledge of professional codes, their values, and their philosophical beliefs about ethics are the cognitive foundations for their decisions regarding whether or not to accept a client for treatment, to help a client achieve his or her stated goals, or to try to help a client rethink the ethics of stated goals. In order to help some clients become members of the ethical community, the counselor may need to engage these clients in dialogue about the ethical ramifications of their stated goals and actions. The counselor needs to approach this therapeutic task in ethical counseling as a challenge to promote higher-quality ethical thinking, which should in turn lead to various positive therapeutic outcomes for the individual and for society as a whole.

Woolfolk and Richardson (1984) comment about the ethical implications of therapeutic goals.

What we find missing in contemporary behavior therapy is not only the absence of any locus of evaluation external to the therapeutic direction prescribed by the client but a failure to allow for any bases for such an evaluation. It has been apparent to poets, philosophers and psychotherapists throughout the ages that an individual's aims in life are often functionally related to their suffering.

Although we second these authors' criticisms, we do not believe the criticism applies only to behavior therapy.

REFERENCES

Aristotle. (1961a). Happiness and virtue. In R. Beck (Ed.), *Perspectives in philosophy: A book of readings* (pp. 60–65). New York: Holt, Rinehart & Winston.

Aristotle. (1961b). Nicomachean ethics. In R. Dewey, F. Gamlich, & N. Loftsgarden (Eds.), *Problems of ethics: A book of readings* (pp. 226–242). New York: Macmillan.

Bourke, V. J. (1951). *Ethics: A textbook in moral philosophy.* New York: Macmillan.

Bruner, E. (1961). The divine imperative. In R. Dewey, F. Gamlich, & N. Loftsgarden (Eds.), *Problems of ethics: A book of readings* (pp. 85–91). New York: Macmillan.

Castell, A. (1943). *An introduction to modern philosophy.* New York: Macmillan.

Clark, G. (1957). *Thales to Dewey: A history of philosophy.* Boston: Houghton Mifflin.

Dewey, J. (1961). Reconstruction in moral conceptions. In R. Dewey, F. Gamlich, & N. Loftsgarden (Eds.), *Problems of ethics: A book of readings* (pp. 295–307). New York: Macmillan.

James, W. (1961). The moral philosopher and the moral life. In R. Dewey, F. Gamlich, & N. Loftsgarden (Eds.), *Problems of ethics: A book of readings* (pp. 262–273). New York: Macmillan.

Kant, I. (1961). Fundamental principles of the metaphysics of morals. In R. Dewey, F. Gamlich, & N. Loftsgarden (Eds.), *Problems of ethics: A book of readings* (pp. 127–151). New York: Macmillan.

Mill, J. S. (1961). Utilitarianism. In R. Dewey, F. Gamlich, & N. Loftsgarden (Eds.), *Problems of ethics: A book of readings* (pp. 178–210). New York: Macmillan.

Steinmeyer, N., Newell, D., & Garcia, L. (1984). *Ethical issues in psychology.* Homewood, IL: Dorsey Press.

Wayland, F. (1961). Conscience or the moral sense. In R. Dewey, F. Gamlich, & N. Loftsgarden (Eds.), *Problems of ethics: A book of readings* (pp. 104–114). New York: Macmillan.

Woolfolk, R., & Richardson, F. (1984). Behavior therapy and the ideology of modernity. *American Psychologist, 39,* 777–786.

Chapter Four

Cognitive Developmental Factors in Ethical Counseling

The cognitive approach to ethical counseling assumes that the major variable that influences the ethical behavior of counseling psychologists is their frame of reference or viewpoint on ethical counseling. The clinician's viewpoint on ethics includes his or her knowledge of professional codes and standards, beliefs about values, and philosophical beliefs about ethical counseling. This chapter describes the role of cognitive developmental processes and structures in the clinician's frame of reference or viewpoint about ethical counseling. In this chapter we examine the clinician's "ways of thinking" about ethical counseling, while the first three chapters had more to do with the content of the clinician's beliefs about ethical counseling.

First, this chapter examines cognitive developmental factors that can affect whether a clinician will recognize and interpret the ethical issues in a professional situation. Social cognitive structures and processes such as role-taking skills, empathy, level of cognitive complexity, and type of cognitive style are possible cognitive factors that can affect the counselor's ability to recognize and identify the ethical issues in a professional situation. Second, this chapter will describe cognitive developmental factors that can influence the counselor's judgments regarding the moral/ethical dilemmas in his or her professional life. Cognitive developmental structures such as the counselor's stage of moral development can affect his or her inferences about fairness and justice; the stage of cognitive/ethical development can affect inferences about truth and certainty.

SOCIAL ROLE-TAKING SKILLS

The first component process in ethical counseling involves the clinician's consideration of how various courses of action in a situation can influence the welfare of concerned individuals. In order to perceive and identify the ethical issues in a situation, a counselor must be able to consider the perspective of others. Social cognition processes and structures, particularly empathy, will play an important role in determining if a clinician views situations as having ethical implications.

One aspect of empathy is the counselor's stage or level of perspective-taking or role-taking. Counselors' role-taking abilities can influence the quality of their inferences about how others see the world and how others view their behavior. In other words, they are able to identify potential moral/ethical conflicts between themselves and other people.

Social role-taking has both cognitive and affective components. The cognitive part of role-taking has to do with thinking about the other person's ways of thinking, while the affective part involves thinking about another's feelings.

Cognitive Role-Taking. Although there are several cognitive developmental models that describe stages of cognitive role-taking, Enright and Lapsely (1980) have identified certain commonalities in them. At the lowest stage, the person does not really consider another person's viewpoint. The assumption is that everyone else has the same viewpoint that he or she has about any given experience. At a later stage, the person begins to realize that others may think differently about a situation. At this point, although the person understands that others have different feelings and thoughts, he or she attributes such differences to the fact that one of them has some information of which the other is ignorant. At the next higher stage, one is able to switch roles and view the world, including oneself, from the other person's perspective. At the highest stage in cognitive role-taking, a person is able to step back from a situation and appreciate how two or more persons' perspectives interact and influence the way each of them thinks and acts.

Each stage or level of cognitive role-taking is seen as a necessary but not a sufficient condition for the development of a parallel stage of ethical reasoning. Thus, the counselor's stage of moral or ethical reasoning is built on an underlying stage of perspective-taking. A counselor's level of perspective-taking is an important cognitive factor in his or her ability to recognize the ethical issues in any given situation. Clearly, a professional who recognizes his or her ethical responsibilities will first have had to consider the thinking of others and appreciate how his or her possible actions could affect the thinking of other people.

Affective Role-Taking and Empathy. Affective role-taking is somewhat different from empathy as traditionally defined. The former has more to do with the counselor's *inferences* about how others feel, whereas the latter has more to do with the counselor's ability to *share* in the feelings of others.

Enright and Lapsley (1980) have described the following developmental sequence in affective role-taking. At first, individuals are aware that others are capable of having emotions and feelings. At the next level, they are capable of anticipating the emotional reactions of others by such primitive psychological tools as projection of their own emotional states, identification with the other person's emotional state, or merely stereotyping others. Such individuals sometimes appear merely to be attributing their own feelings to others. At a higher stage, individuals are able to assume multiple points of view relative to the affective states of others. They are aware of possible present and past conditions that could be influencing how the other person feels, and they understand the environmental factors that can influence feelings.

As counselors advance to higher levels of affective role-taking and/ or cognitive role-taking, we would expect them to be less egocentric and to use complex thinking about the feelings of others and the possible reasons for their feelings. At higher levels of affective role-taking, counselors will consider psychological, social, and historical causes for others' feelings. As a result, they will be less apt to jump to conclusions about why people feel as they do about them or other people in their lives. Counselors with higher levels of affective role-taking will always be more willing to reconsider or reevaluate their initial feelings about others.

In order to identify the ethical issues in a professional situation, the counselor needs to be willing to consider the feelings of others. Without the presence of this kind of concern for the feelings of others, the ethical issues in any situation probably will not be viewed as ethical or moral imperatives (see Hoffman, 1979).

A counselor's empathic feelings or ability to shape the feelings of others will reflect his or her level of cognitive and affective role-taking as well as the kinds of attributions that the counselor makes about the feelings and thoughts of others (Selman, 1980; Shantz, 1975).

Empathy skills seem to follow a cognitive developmental sequence in which the individual's responsiveness to the feelings and views of others changes and becomes more differentiated and integrated. The first stage in empathy probably involves little more than vague feelings about others. In the higher stages, the person becomes capable of increasingly complex and abstract responses to the conditions of others. Probably the highest stage in empathy occurs when a person is capable of a responsiveness to the life experiences of others and to how these experiences contributed to the person's present condition or status.

COGNITIVE COMPLEXITY AND COGNITIVE STYLE

The professional counselor's awareness of the ethical issues in a professional situation can also be influenced by his or her level of cognitive complexity and cognitive style. One way of describing cognitive complexity is to identify the number and organization of constructs, propositions, and schemata that a person uses to interpret and make sense of a situation (Kelly, 1955). A person at a higher level of cognitive complexity is capable of using more constructs to describe other people, and is capable of identifying and describing how these various constructs are related to each other. A person's constructs are the bipolar dimensions of judgment, such as good–bad, and they are the elements of the counselor's knowledge system which are used to anticipate future events. In other words, the number and quality of the counselor's constructs about ethics will influence his or her perception and discrimination of the ethical issues in any professional situation. As a consequence, the complexity of the counselor's construct system can be an important cognitive factor that influences his or her inferences about the ethical implications of professional actions.

Another cognitive structure that can affect the counselor's inferences about the ethical issues in a professional situation is his or her cognitive style. Witkin and Goodenough (1977) have described how a person's degree of field dependence/independence (a cognitive style) is related to interpersonal behavior. This type of cognitive style reflects the level of cognitive differentiation of self from the environment and the relative independence of the individual's psychological processes from concrete referents in the physical environment. Field dependence/independence is a cognitive component that can influence the degree to which counselors rely on internal versus external cues to identify and label the ethical issues in a situation. However, the potential relationship between field dependence and a counselor's awareness of ethical issues is not clear.

In a fairly ambiguous professional situation, it might be argued that field-dependent counselors will rely more on the criteria used by others to identify the salient ethical issues. Consequently, these counselors might be found to be very concerned about how their behavior is seen by others, and as a result of this strong concern about social impressions, they might be less empathic to deviant individuals who are not part of mainstream society. These field-dependent counselors might also be found to be less apt to identify and label ethical issues in a professional situation that involves conflicts between a client and the dominant norms of the counselor's own reference groups or norm groups. On the other hand, it could be argued that since field-dependent counselors' identification of ethical issues is more influenced by social contextual cues than would be the case for field-independent counselors, the field-dependent counselors might be more empathic and responsive toward other people. Still, it is also possible that field-independent counselors, since they are more likely to be influenced by internal cues such as intellectual principles, would be more empathic to a wider variety of people when their rights appear to have been violated by mainstream society. As you can see, the relationship between field dependence/independence of counselors and their awareness of ethical issues in professional situations is undoubtedly complex.

Cognitive Development

Cognitive development is a way of describing how systematic changes occur in the thinking of counselors when they are dealing with various kinds of moral/ethical dilemmas in their professional lives (Kohlberg, 1958, 1984). In cognitive development, there are two complementary processes called assimilation and accommodation. Assimilation occurs when the clinician tries to change the environment or the professional situation to fit his or her present or existing cognitive structures. Accommodation describes a process whereby the counselor modifies his or her present cognitive structures about ethical counseling to deal with the environment or the professional situation. The interaction between accommodation and assimilation creates a dynamic balance, and cognitive development is seen to occur when and if there is some degree of cognitive disequilibrium and emotional arousal due to an imbalance in these two processes. Developmental stages can be described as periods or indices of relative balance between the assimilation and accommodation processes. Clearly, there will not be developmental changes in thinking about ethical counseling unless, first, a counselor can at least partly understand issues in a professional situation (assimilation) from his or her present frame of reference about ethics and, second, he or she simultaneously experiences some degree of uncertainty about the ethical implications or issues in the situation. A counselor's level of uncertainty about potential ethical issues in a situation can be considered a rough index of cognitive arousal and as such should be viewed as a potentially positive factor that could lead to higher stages of ethical reasoning.

Generally, cognitive developmental theorists consider development as sequential and invariant. Although cultural factors may speed up, slow down, or even stop development, these factors cannot change the sequence or order of development. Certainly, a cognitive/developmental model is not value-neutral. A criterion of healthiness or maturity is openly defined as the "end point," and the stages are seen as qualitatively different, with higher stages being "better" in that they provide an individual with more complex and more adequate skills to interact effectively with the environment. Higher-stage thinking represents a more internally consistent and more stable means of interacting with the environment than does a lower stage.

The cognitive developmental models do not assume that development is automatic. A person develops through a balance of challenges and support. Ethical issues present cognitive dilemmas that upset the stability of the counselor's personality and create emotional arousal that may be experienced as stress. If present or existing modes of viewing or thinking do not work (assimilation), a counselor may be forced to find new ways of thinking about the ethical issues in a dilemma (accomodation). However, if the emotional arousal is too great, the counselor may appear resistant and defensive. Strong emotional arousal may even contribute to excessive defensiveness and lack of awareness of the ethical issues in a professional situation.

In order to develop higher-stage ethical reasoning, the clinician has to have a positive view of his or her level of emotional arousal associated with cognitive uncertainty about ethical issues, be willing to engage in exploratory behavior regarding ethical issues, and be willing to maintain a nonjudgmental attitude toward the views of others. We want to encourage our readers to view moral/ethical issues, although sometimes stressful, as having the potential to influence positively their own level of personal development.

MODELS OF MORAL JUDGMENT

Ethical counselors who have identified ethical issues then must consider the relevance of various moral/ethical criteria for resolving the potential conflicts between themselves and others. The concepts of justice, fairness, and concern for others, as well as one's concept of ideal social relationships, will influence the quality of reasoning in the moral/ethical judgment process in ethical counseling. We will argue that counselors differ in their stages of reasoning about the appropriate resolution of moral/ethical dilemmas and that these differences are reflected in the cognitive developmental models presented here.

Moral judgment development describes stages of thinking and resultant inferences about the fairness and appropriateness of different role expectations regarding rights and responsibilities. Cognitive/ethical development describes stages of thinking and resultant inferences about "truth" and "certainty" of information provided by others. These two types of inferences play a major part in ethical counseling.

Morality of Acting

Kohlberg (1984) assumes that the development of moral judgment reflects general cognitive development and is the outcome of an active social process involving experiences with peers and exposure to higher stages of moral reasoning. Experiences that broaden an individual's perspective on authority and increase role-taking skills are assumed to facilitate higher levels of moral reasoning.

Lawrence Kohlberg's model of moral judgment development is based on earlier work by Piaget as well as Baldwin (Kohlberg, 1984). Piaget ([1932] 1948, 1965) described the development of moral judgment from preschool years through middle childhood and up to the beginning of adolescence. His three stages in moral development were (a) pre-moral, (b) heteronomous, and (c) autonomous. Two distinct types of morality identified in childhood were the morality of constraint (i.e., "following rules is right") and the morality of cooperation (i.e., "social reciprocity and mutual respect is right"). For Piaget, childhood morality involved understanding the values of cooperation as well as having a sense of justice. Seemingly, moral maturity was to be reached when the individual was capable of autonomous reasoning about social rules, which occurs roughly at about 12 years of age.

Lawrence Kohlberg's interest was in adolescent moral judgment development. His original work (Kohlberg & Kramer, 1969) was based on a sample of 72 boys, ages 10 to 16 years, whose development was followed at 3-year intervals. Kohlberg administered a series of moral dilemmas in which he presented conflicts between conformity to authority and a utilitarian or "greatest good" approach to situational values and social value objects. For example, the conflicts included the value of life versus the value of property, the value of obedience versus that of keeping promises, respect for the individual versus concern for group welfare. Based on the boys' conceptions of such ideas as life, law, property, authority, punishment, and conscience, he identified six developmental types of value orientations which he called (a) Obedience and Punishment, (b) Naively Egotistic, (c) Good Boy, (d) Authority and Social Order Maintenance, (e) Contractual/Legalistic, and (f) Conscience or Principles. These types then provided the basis for his six stages of moral reasoning.

The developmental progression is from an initial preconventional level, through the conventional level to a postconventional level. These levels involve an expansion in moral perspective and reflect hierarchical reorganizations of the person's ways of thinking about justice. The three levels describe three differentiated and integrated understandings of the concepts of rights, justice, and fairness.

What follows is a brief description of the three levels and six stages in the Kohlberg model (see Kohlberg, 1984).

At the preconventional level, the person is responsive to cultural rules and labels regarding right and wrong or good and bad. However, these labels are interpreted very specifically in terms of concrete consequences such as punishment or reward as well as the physical power of the person who is demanding that certain rules should be followed. At this level there are the following two stages:

1. *Punishment and obedience orientation.* The physical consequences of actions determine their goodness or badness. To avoid punishment and to defer to power are values in their own right.
2. *Instrumental-relativist orientation.* Right actions are those actions that satisfy one's own needs and sometimes the needs of others. Justice is simply reciprocity or equal exchange. The key factor in moral judgments is "looking out for number one."

At the conventional level, the individual values social conformity and maintenance of the expectations of the family, group, or nation. A person should conform and be loyal to the social order. At this level there are the following two stages:

3. *Interpersonal concordance or "good boy–nice girl" orientation.* Good behavior is that which pleases or helps others and is approved by them. Behavior is frequently judged by intention. For example, he or she means well.
4. *Authority and social order maintenance orientation.* Values at this stage emphasize authority, fixed rules and the maintenance of the social order.

At the post-conventional or principled level, the individual has defined moral values and principles that have validity apart from the authority of any specific groups holding to them or apart from an individual's identification with these groups. At this level there are the following two stages:

5. *The social contract legalistic orientation.* Right actions are defined in terms of general individual rights and in terms of standards that have been critically examined and agreed on by the whole society. Aside from what is constitutionally and democratically agreed on, right is a matter of personal values and opinions.
6. *The universal ethical principle orientation.* Right actions are defined by a decision of conscience in accord with self-chosen ethical principles that are logically comprehensive, universal, and consistent. These are universal principles of justice, the reciprocity and equality of human rights, and respect for the dignity of human beings as individuals.

Moral maturity, or the capacity for principled thinking, has been found to be attained by very few people. However, individuals who attain moral maturity usually do so in their late adolescence or early adulthood. Somewhat surprisingly, during the same age period the stability of development appears to be interrupted. Between late high school and the second or third year of college, 20% of Kohlberg's sample seemed to regress in moral maturity scores (Kohlberg, 1984). College sophomores were found to be the sole exception to the generalization that change in moral reasoning is usually forward and sequential. The regressors temporarily abandoned higher stages of moral reasoning and reverted back to Stage 2, "hedonistic relativism." However, Kohlberg reported that by age 25 all regressors returned to the higher stages of moral reasoning.

In a recent reformulation of Stage 6, as the end point in his model of moral judgment (Kohlberg, Boyd, & Levine, 1985), Kohlberg clarifies the role of principles and attitudes in defining the moral view of Stage 6 thinkers. The central theme for these Stage 6 people is an attitude of "respect for persons" that reflects a dual concern for the principles of justice and beneficence. The former has principally to do with distributing goods equitably, whereas the latter is concerned more with the maximal promoting of the general welfare or the general good. In Stage 6 thinking, the moral point of view requires individuals to resolve moral conflicts through dialogue and consensus, and this dialogue should be characterized by an attitude of sympathy, reciprocal role-taking, and "universability." The participants' goals should at all times reflect the attitude of "respect for persons."

Simply stated, moral judgment as viewed by Kohlberg has to do with how people think or reason about moral problems. The emphasis is on problem-solving, and the differences between the higher and lower stages reflect differences in the quality of thinking and conceptualization of the issues in the problem. Stages represent different patterns in people's thinking as well as differences in problem-solving skills.

Morality of Judging

James Rest (1979) extended Kohlberg's model, which focuses on the morality of the actor to include the morality of the judge. The Kohlberg method of assessment clearly emphasizes the actor's thinking in moral dilemmas, whereas Rest's measure of moral judgment development, called the Defining Issues Test, is concerned with people's judgments about the important issues in various moral dilemmas. The assumption is that a person's choice of important issues reflects different stages in moral reasoning.

Rest (1979) also differs from Kohlberg in that he uses a continuous variable rather than a stage typology score to index moral development. For him, the key question in moral judgment is not "What stage is a person in?" but rather, "To what extent and under what conditions does a person manifest various types or organizations of thinking?" (p. 63) He and his colleagues have found that people fluctuate in their use of various structures or stages of thinking. For example, first they may use a stage of thinking very seldom, while later they may use the stage fairly consistently in appropriate situations. Research by Rest and his colleagues does not support the assumption that moral development is a step-by-step vertical process through the stages. Consequently, he does not characterize individuals using a single stage score. Rather, he describes a person as having advanced levels of Stage 3, moderate levels of Stage 4, modest levels of Stage 5, and/or a percentage of "principled thinking."

Rest's model of moral judgment development also has six stages, with major characteristics very similar to Kohlberg's. However, in Rest's scheme, the underlying variable is a concept of ideal social cooperation. Moral rules and principles are viewed as modes of regulating the basic relationships among people in terms of allocating social rights and responsibilities (Rest, 1979). In order to have a stable system of social cooperation, individuals must recognize the norms of social behavior and accept and support the system. Sociomoral development begins with rudimentary concepts of shared expectations (norms are demands of powerful figures) and culminates in a concept of mutual expectations founded on a logical analysis of the requirements of an ideal system of cooperation.

In his model Rest uses two factors in defining six stages of thinking about social cooperation: (1) how mutual expectations among cooperating individuals are established, and (2) how the interests of individuals are to be balanced. Rest's stages of moral judgment are summarized briefly in Table 4.1.

Women's Moral Development

Gilligan (1977) criticized Kohlberg's model of moral judgment as not representative of the concerns and experiences of women. The argument is that women's concepts of morality focus more on con-

TABLE 4.1 Rest's Stages of Moral Judgment

Stage	Coordination of expectations about actions (how rules are known and shared)	Schemes of balancing interests (how equilibrium is achieved)	Central concept for determining moral rights and responsibilities
Stage 1	The caretaker makes known certain demands on the child's behavior.	The child does not share in making rules, but understands that obedience will bring freedom from punishment.	The morality of obedience: "Do what you're told."
Stage 2	Although each person is understood to have his own interests, an exchange of favors might be decided.	If each party sees something to gain in an exchange, then both want to reciprocate.	The morality of instrumental egoism and simple exchange: "Let's make a deal."
Stage 3	Through reciprocal role-taking, individuals attain a mutual understanding about each other and the on-going pattern of their interactions.	Friendship relationships establish a stabilized and enduring scheme of cooperation. Each party anticipates the feelings, needs, and wants of the other and acts in the other's welfare.	The morality of interpersonal concordance: "Be considerate, nice, and kind, and you'll get along with people."
Stage 4	All members of society know what is expected of them through public institutionalized law.	Unless a society-wide system of cooperation is established and stabilized, no individual can really make plans. Each person should follow the law and do his particular job, anticipating that other people will also fulfill their responsibilities.	The morality of law and duty to the social order: "Everyone in society is obligated and protected by the law."

Stage 5	Formal procedures are institutionalized for making laws, which one anticipates rational people would accept.	Law-making procedures are devised so that they reflect the general will of the people, at the same time insuring certain basic rights to all. With each person having a say in the decision process, each will see that his interests are maximized while at the same time having a basis for making claims on other people.	The morality of societal consensus: "You are obligated by whatever arrangements are agreed to by due process procedures."
Stage 6	The logical requirements of non-arbitrary cooperation among rational, equal, and impartial people are taken as ideal criteria for social organization which one anticipates rational people would accept.	A scheme of cooperation that negates or neutralizes all arbitrary distribution of rights and responsibilities is the most equilibrated, for such system is maximizing the simultaneous benefit to each member so that any deviation from these rules would advantage some members at the expense of others.	The morality of non-arbitrary social cooperation: "How rational and impartial people would organize cooperation is moral."

From Rest (1979), with permission.

siderations of care and response to others while men's concepts of morality have more to do with considerations of justice and individual rights.

Gilligan's model of women's moral development follows a three-level progression: (1) egocentric, (2) societal, and (3) universal. A brief description of each level follows:

Level 1: Orientation to Individual Survival. The focus is on the self, and her needs are the sole object of concern. She is constrained by her lack of power. Morality is viewed as the sanctions imposed on her by society. *Should* and *would* are not differentiated.

First Transition: From Selfishness to Responsibility. The transitional issue is one of attachment or connection to others. There is an emergent conflict between what one wishes and what are considered to be necessities. The "selfishness" of willful decision is counterposed to the "responsibility" of moral choices. The transition signals an enhancement in self-worth and a concept of self that includes the possibility of "doing the right thing." The concept of responsibility is the basis for a new equilibrium between self and others.

Level 2: Goodness as Self-Sacrifice. Moral judgment is based on shared norms and expectations. Social values are adopted as her own. Taking care of and protecting others is highly valued. Concern for the feelings of others is very important. Goodness is seen as self-sacrifice. She considers herself to be responsible for the actions of others, and she holds others responsible for the choices she makes. The need for approval is tied to the wish to care for and help others.

Second Transition: From Goodness to Truth. The woman reconsiders the relationship between self and others and starts to question the logic of self-sacrifice in the service of a morality of care. The key issue is whether she also can consider her own needs as part of her concepts of care and concern. Honesty and truth become the important criterion for judgments. Morality needs to consider the realities of intentions and consequences.

It is important to be responsible to yourself and thus to be "honest" and "real." She questions whether it is ever right to hurt or harm oneself.

Level 3: The Morality of Nonviolence. Nonviolence is a principle governing all moral judgment. There is a moral equality between herself and others. Care is a universal obligation that includes responsibility for choices.

Her concept of a good person includes directness and honesty.

You should be willing to express and take responsibility for your moral judgments. Responsibility for care includes self and others. The obligation not to hurt is seen as a universal guide to moral action.

Gilligan's model emphasizes a morality of responsibility, compared to Kohlberg's model, which seemingly has more emphasis on rights. The moral imperative for women is "to care" and "take responsibility" to discern and alleviate the real troubles of the world. In contrast, the moral imperative for men would seem to be an injunction to respect the rights of others.

Adult Morality

In discussing adult morality, Gilligan and Murphy (1979) criticize Kohlberg's model because it is based on reasoning about hypothetical problems rather than "real-life" problems. They argue that moral reasoning in its real-life contexts depends on cognitive structures that are not derived solely from formal logic. For them, the transition from adolescent to adult moral development involves the confrontation between *contextual relativism* and *hypothetical moral reasoning*. For the adult, moral judgment involves both the context of justice and the universal logic of fairness as well as a context of compassion and consideration for the particular consequences for actual people involved. The right moral judgment has to consider the actuality of time and place. Gilligan and Murphy (1979) report research indicating that the shift to a dual context form of reasoning is very prominent in a number of subjects between 22 and 27 years. For them, the problem of judgment occurs in two contexts that frame different aspects of the moral problem: the context of justice, in which a person articulates the universal logic of fairness and reciprocity, and the context of compassion, in which a person focuses on the particular consequences for actual people. The resolution combines the absolute logic of a system of moral justification with a probabilistic contextual assessment of the likely consequences of choices.

Because of the sex bias in Kohlberg's model, Gilligan and Murphy (1979) maintain that his concept of adult morality is overly rational. The argument regarding the nature of adult morality is based on an underlying assumption that there is a stage of postconventional thought. Kramer (1983) has suggested that postformal thinkers display an understanding of the nonabsolute, relative nature of knowledge. For them, moral/ethical knowledge would be temporarily true and not universally fixed. Rybash, Roodin, and Hoyer (1986) recommend that an adult concept of morality needs to reflect (a) an ability to recognize new contexts for applying moral principles and (b) an ability to construct new moral principles as contexts change and existing principles become outmoded.

Cognitive Ethical Development

William Perry (1968) has described a model of intellectual and ethical development. His scheme of development involves sequential interpretations of the meaning of truth and certainty and emphasizes the transitions between positions rather than stages. Cognitive/ethical development starts from a naive concept of objective truth to an increased awareness that a search for the single "right answer" is futile. Perry adds an advanced period of cognitive development to Piaget's model. During this latter stage, thinking is transformed from the moral environment to the ethical, from the formal to the existential.

The Perry model describes four major positions in thinking about the nature of knowledge, truth, and values (see Table 4.2).

"Dualism" is the first position and involves the use of discrete, concrete, and absolute categories to understand the world and what is important. Knowledge exists in an absolute sense. Individuals should be able to know the truth directly. Alternative explanations are difficult to understand and/or accept.

The next position is called "multiplicity" and involves the recognition of multiple perspectives and multiple answers. Points of view cannot be evaluated because all opinions are equally valid. Value neutrality is a banner and a slogan for individuals in this position.

A third position, labeled "relativism," brings a recognition that knowledge is contextual and that information and competing ideas need to be evaluated on the basis of *evidence.* The context for a point of view becomes a significant factor in an individual's thinking. Opinions are analyzed and compared using criteria such as sources of information, logic of arguments, and rules of evidence.

The final position involves "commitments within relativism," and these provide an affirmation of one's identity in a pluralistic world. Individuals recognize the diversity in their lives. However, they realize that they must still make decisions and judgments in an uncertain world.

According to Perry, in order to develop cognitively, people must confront what appear to be inconsistent and contradictory views

TABLE 4.2 Perry Scheme of Cognitive and Ethical Development

Position 1	Authorities know, and if we work hard, read every word, and learn Right Answers, all will be well.
Transition	But what about those Others I hear about? And different opinions? And Uncertainties? Some of our own Authorities disagree with each other or don't seem to know, and some give us problems instead of Answers.
Position 2	True Authorities must be Right, the others are frauds. We remain Right. Others must be different and Wrong. Good Authorities give us problems so we can learn to find the Right Answer by our own independent thought.
Transition	But even Good Authorities admit they don't know all the answers *yet!*
Position 3	Then some uncertainties and different opinions are real and legitimate *temporarily*, even for Authorities. They're working on them to get to the Truth.
Transition	But there are *so many* things they don't know the Answers to! And they won't for a long time.
Position 4a	Where Authorities don't know the Right Answers, everyone has a right to his own opinion; no one is wrong!
Transition (and/or)	But some of my friends ask me to support my opinions with facts and reasons.
Transition	Then what right have They to grade us? About what?
Position 4b	In certain courses Authorities are not asking for the Right Answer; They want us to *think* about things in a certain way, *supporting* opinion with data. That's what they grade us on.
Transition	But this "way" seems to *work* in most courses, and even outside them.
Position 5	Then *all* thinking must be like this, even for Them. Everything is relative but not equally valid. You have to understand how each context works. Theories are not Truth but metaphors to interpret data with. You have to think about your thinking.
Transition	But if everything is relative, am I relative too? How can I know I'm making the Right Choice?
Position 6	I see I'm going to have to make my own decisions in an uncertain world with no one to tell me I'm Right.
Transition	I'm lost if I don't. When I decide on my career (or marriage or values) everything will straighten out.
Position 7	Well, I've made my first Commitment!
Transition	Why didn't that settle everything?
Position 8	I've made several commitments. I've got to balance them— how many, how deep? How certain, how tentative?
Transition	Things are getting contradictory. I can't make logical sense out of life's dilemmas.
Position 9	This is how life will be. I must be wholehearted while tentative, fight for my values yet respect others, believe my deepest values right yet be ready to learn. I see that I shall be retracing this whole journey over and over—but, I hope, more wisely.

about right or correct ideas and actions. When people are forced to deal with these inconsistent and contradictory views, they often experience emotional arousal, which they then attempt to reduce through the complementary processes of accommodation and assimilation. Perry describes these experiences as transitions that influence whether or not individuals develop new ways of thinking about their experiences.

For Perry, there are three alternatives to forward movement. *Temporizing* is the postponement of movement for a year or more. *Escape* involves alienation and abandonment of responsibility. Multiplicity can be used as a reason for avoiding intellectual commitments, and relativism can be used as the reason for lack of actions. The third alternative, *Retreat*, involves avoiding complexity and ambivalence by a regression to dualism.

The transitions described in Table 4.2 reflect the interaction of assimilation and accomodation processes. In this model the assimilation processes involve altering the meaning of experiences in order to reduce their dissonance with the individual's present *meaning structures* regarding truth and certainty, while the accommodation process involves a rethinking of these cognitive *meaning structures* to reduce dissonance. For example, relativistic thinking is first perceived as a special case of dualistic thinking of "what they want." Of necessity, this type of assimilation thinking will force a change or accommodation of fundamental assumptions. The intellectual shift is from viewing correctness as "what is wanted" to viewing correctness as "the way something is wanted."

In Perry's model the highest stage of cognitive/ethical development reflects an appreciation for the central role of dialectical processes in thought and in action. Persons are able to think and act with an awareness that they cannot be certain either that their beliefs are "certainly true" or that their actions are "certainly right." On the basis of Perry's model, we would contend that ethical counseling of necessity has to be free of dogmatism.

CONCLUSION

This chapter presents a cognitive developmental perspective on morality and ethics. This perspective deals with the elusive aspects of quality of thinking and judgments. The argument, simply stated, is that ethical counseling varies depending on *how* clinicians think as well as *what* clinicians think. The American Psychological

Association code of ethics and the American Association for Counseling and Development code of ethics reflect important knowledge to be used in Ethical Counseling, still these documents are interpreted and applied in particular professional situations. The professional counselor is involved in "information processing," and using his or her cognitive rules to interpret and identify ethical issues, and then to make ethical judgments. We hold that ethical and moral judgments are a function of both cognitive information and ways of thinking that influence the professional person's awareness of ethical issues and his or her judgments about them. Ethical counseling is not simply the mechanical application of professional ethical codes. Even though these codes play an important role in determining the ethical actions and judgments of counselors, this chapter has identified and described cognitive development components in information processing that also play a role in ethical counseling.

A major reason for counselors to understand the role of cognitive/ developmental factors in ethical thinking is that they often confront complex situations in which each of several participants thinks very differently about moral and ethical issues. For instance, in a family counseling situation the counselor might encounter an ethical dilemma that is viewed very differently by the parents and the children. Their comments may be characterized by lack of empathy, cognitive simplicity, and conflicts about moral criteria. The counselor's ethical judgments then need to consider the quality of thinking used by his or her clients as well as the content of their statements.

In the following chapters we will discuss various professional ethical issues. The relevant professional ethical principles and standards will be described. The reader will be encouraged to consider these issues actively by referring to specific situations and then to develop arguments in support of different moral/ethical interpretations and actions.

REFERENCES

Enright, R., & Lapsley, O. (1980). Social role taking: A review of the constructs, measures, and measurement procedures. *Review of Educational Research, 50,* 647–674.

Gilligan, C. (1977). In a different voice: Women's conception of the self and of morality. *Harvard Education Review, 47,* 481–517.

Gilligan, C., & Murphy, J. (1979). Development from adolescence to adulthood: The philosopher and the dilemma of the fact. In W. Damon (Ed.), *New directions for child development* (pp. 5, 85–100). San Francisco: Jossey Bass.

Hoffman, M. L. (1979). Development of moral thought, feeling and behavior. *American Psychologist, 34,* 958–966.

Kelly, G. *The psychology of personal constructs.* New York: W. W. Norton.

Kohlberg, L. (1958). *The development of modes of moral thinking and choices in the years 10–16.* Unpublished doctoral dissertation, University of Chicago.

Kohlberg, L. (1984). *The psychology of moral development: The nature and validity of moral stages.* San Francisco: Harper and Row.

Kohlberg, L., Boyd, D., & Levine, C. (1985). *The return of stage 6: Its principal and its moral point of view* (mimeo).

Kohlberg, L., & Kramer, R. (1969). Continuities and discontinuities in childhood and adult moral development. *Human Development, 12,* 93–120.

Kramer, D. (1983). Post-formal operations? A need for further conceptualization. *Human Development, 26,* 91–105.

Perry, W. (1968). *Forms of intellectual and ethical development in the college years: A scheme.* New York: Holt, Rinehart and Winston.

Piaget, J. (1948, 1965). *The moral judgment of the child.* Glencoe, IL: Free Press. (Original work published 1932).

Rest, J. (1979). *Development in judging moral issues.* Minneapolis: University of Minnesota Press.

Rybash, J., Roodin, P., & Hoyer, W. (1986). Adult morality: A neo-Piagetian perspective on cognition and affect. *The Genetic Epistemologist, 14*(2), 24–29.

Selman, R. (1980). *The growth of interpersonal understanding.* New York: Academic Press.

Shantz, C. (1975). *The development of social cognition* (Review of Child Development Research 4). Chicago: University of Chicago Press.

Witkin, H. A., & Goodenough, O. R. (1977). Field dependence and interpersonal behavior. *Psychological Bulletin, 84,* 661–689.

II
Ethical Counseling: Major Professional Issues

One reason for the appeal of paternalistic lies is that they, unlike so much deception, are felt to be without bias and told in a disinterested wish to be helpful to fellow human beings in need. On closer examination, however, this objectivity and disinterest are often found to be spurious. The benevolent motives claimed by liars are then seen to be mixed with many others much less altruistic—the fear of confrontation which would accompany a more outspoken acknowledgement of the liar's feelings and intentions; the desire to avoid setting in motion great pressures to change, as where addiction or infidelity are no longer concealed; the urge to maintain the power that comes with duping others (never greater than when those lied to are defenseless or in need of care). These are motives of self-protection and of manipulation, of wanting to retain control over a situation and to remain a free agent. So long as the liar does not see them clearly, his judgment that his lies are altruistic and thus excused is itself biased and unreliable.

—S. Bok, *Lying: Moral Choice in Public and Private Life*

Chapter Five

The Application of Ethical Principles in Clinical Practice

Nothing is more central to the practice of counseling and psychotherapy than *trust*. Counseling, by its very nature, involves a relationship built on mutual confidence, respect, and consideration. The progress of clinical work almost invariably involves the client in an active process of self-exploration and self-disclosure. In this process the client usually becomes progressively more vulnerable and is asked to risk more and more in terms of dropping facades and defenses and opening himself or herself both to rigorous self-examination and to the view of the clinician who is, after all, a comparative stranger. Much of the art of clinical interviewing is directed toward helping the client to proceed with this process of self-exploration and self-disclosure with feelings of relative safety and comfort.

To a considerable degree, however, the clinician not only depends on his or her *own* clinical skills and communication of expertness, attractiveness, and trustworthiness but also draws on the generalized expectations of trustworthiness, expertness, and integrity that the client brings to the counseling situation from his or her own experiences as a member of the larger society.

Those hard-won expectations of trust, confidence, and faith in both the competence and ethical integrity of counselors are earned not solely by any individual clinician, no matter how skilled or committed, but are, rather, the product of many years of commitment, concern, and service provided by an entire profession.

The very concept of a profession is one that is often used loosely and ambiguously by those who seek the status, power, and autonomy that the title of "professional" tends to imply. As a matter of fact, however, professionalism is not a function of any of the myriad status symbols that are usually associated with the term. Professionals do not achieve their identities in terms of the size of the fees they charge, the number of degrees or diplomas hanging on their office walls, or whether they practice privately or function within institutional settings. These kinds of superficial characteristics are trivial and inconsequential aspects of professional identity. The reality is that all real professions arise out of and are distinguished by a *public trust.*

This public trust that defines and distinguishes any profession is fragile and perhaps ephemeral. It is, however, the most important and precious asset possessed by any professional practitioner. It is public respect and trust, of course, that brings clients to any clinician, or other professional, in the first place. Without such public confidence there would soon be no clients to counsel.

Equally important is the fact that the autonomy and independence in judgment and action that characterizes professional practice arises out of public trust, respect, and confidence in the clinician as a competent, committed, and deeply ethical person.

This kind of public trust is neither quickly nor easily won. It accumulates slowly out of the shared experiences of people. It can, however, be eroded very quickly and, as it is diminished, produce catastrophic consequences for professionals themselves. We witness today a genuine crisis in the profession of medicine brought on in some degree by an erosion in public esteem and confidence. As this crisis in confidence is translated into an epidemic of malpractice litigation, some physicians are brought to the brink of financial ruin, and the professional practice of medicine is actually threatened.

As we noted, all professional practice emerges out of and is sustained by the perceptions and expectations of the public about the profession. As we saw in Chapter 1, three very crucial sets of perceptions are central to public trust. We will elaborate further on each of these "core expectations" below.

The Expectation of Competence

Perhaps the most central and compelling basis for trust in any profession is the perception of *competence*. Professionals are initially identified, sought after, and finally accorded respect primarily because they are perceived to have special, useful, and current knowledge and expertise not found in the general population. This competence is usually seen to arise out of special preparation, experience, and ability. Such competence is generally attested to by formal credentials such as advanced degrees, licenses, or certificates. Usually, it is also affirmed by membership in appropriate professional associations or societies. In other words, one professional's competence is affirmed by the acceptance, respect, and collegiality accorded to him or her by other professionals.

Obviously, when incompetent, inexpert, or unqualified practitioners are allowed to enter, remain in, or pass themselves off as members of a profession, the public's perception of competence will eventually be eroded, and every member of that profession is damaged or diminished to some degree.

For this reason, then, most professional groups seek to influence or even to control entry into the profession. This is often done through the accreditation of training programs by professional associations and by lobbying for licensure or certification of all practitioners who represent themselves as members of the profession.

The Expectation of Professional Regulation

The second major expectation out of which public trust for professionals grows is that professionals and professional practice are systematically regulated for the *public's* interest and protection. Generally, this set of expectations is twofold. First, there is the expectation that public regulation will occur. This expectation is met through the operation of licensing boards, the monitoring of training programs by departments of education, requirements for entry examinations for hiring, and other governmental regulations.

In addition to such public or governmental regulation, however, public confidence also rests on the belief that professionals, individually and through their associations, will regulate or police themselves in the public interest.

Such self-regulation is accomplished through the development, dissemination and enforcement of ethical codes and statements of standards for practice by professional associations. These associations, with the cooperation of their individual members, take responsibility for protecting the public from unethical, incompetent, or irresponsible practitioners. We examined briefly these standards, or "ethical beliefs," earlier.

Obviously, the ethical principles and professional standards promulgated by such associations do not have the force of law. They use only the sanctions of suspension or expulsion of members from the association itself to ensure compliance. When, however, a professional association expels a member unwilling to abide by the ethical principles and standards for practice defined by its members, that profession demonstrates its commitment to protect the public interest as well as its own integrity.

The Expectation of Public Service

The third and in many ways the most fragile set of public expectations that sustains professional practice is the belief that professionals are motivated to provide a public service; in other words, that they are dedicated to a set of values that transcends their own monetary interests or needs for power and status.

This set of expectations is affirmed or discredited in the eyes of the public by the behavior of individuals, practitioners, and professional associations. When professional groups seek solely to enhance their own financial interests through engaging in destructive competition or monopolistic practices in regard to other professions, they obviously undermine public confidence. When such groups lobby for public policies that are merely designed to enhance their own economic positions, they similarly destroy the perception of commitment to public service.

So too, when individual practitioners charge excessive or unfair fees, terminate clients prematurely because of inability to pay, or tailor delivery systems to reach only the most affluent or advantaged members of the community, they destroy their image of professionalism and become simply another group of entrepreneurs preoccupied with self-enrichment.

PRINCIPLES OF ETHICAL PRACTICE

We noted above that because professionals have such a high stake in preserving and enhancing the trust extended to them, they seek, through professional associations, to set ethical standards or codes of conduct for their members. These ethical codes provide both practitioners and the public with a way of understanding the duties, responsibilities, and obligations undertaken by the profession. When the ethical responsibilities and obligations reflected in such codes or standards are ignored or flouted, the professional association can act to protect the welfare of the public and its own reputation.

In a sense, then, an ethical code is a set of principles laid down by a profession to guide its members in discharging their duties as professionals. Because many of the situations and relationships confronting professional counselors are very complex, ethical codes for clinicians are not easy and simple either to devise or to interpret. Too often they are interpreted narrowly as "laws" or rules to be followed mechanically rather than as broad guiding principles.

The most useful approach to codifying ethical behavior in the human services professions is to identify and clarify a set of basic *general principles* that can be applied in a wide range of specific professional relationships and clinical situations.

As we saw earlier, the American Psychological Association (1981) has developed such a set of principles to guide its members in professional practice. These principles are very basic and tend also to be reflected in the ethical codes established by other professional associations of counselors such as the American Association for Counseling and Development (in 1984) and the American Association for Marriage and Family Therapy (in 1974).

We will utilize the set of ethical principles developed by the American Psychological Association as the framework for the ensuing discussion. These principles, which we discussed briefly earlier, will be described in terms of their implications for general clinical practice, whether by counseling psychologists or other professional practitioners.

These ethical principles must always be interpreted within the context of the profession's deep commitment to providing services to individuals in a democratic society. They reflect deeply held values and commitments and are not seen as narrowly defined rules or laws to be obeyed blindly or arbitrarily.

Responsibility

Perhaps the paramount and most important ethical principle relevant to counseling practice is represented in the concept of professional responsibility. Professionals, as we saw, are identified by the bestowal of public trust. This trust or confidence in turn creates for the professional a heavy set of responsibilities. Public trust is given to the individual practitioner. The responsibilities that follow from that trust cannot be delegated to others. Supervisors, employing institutions, or even government agencies can never relieve the clinician from his or her own professional responsibilities.

Professional counselors make judgments, provide services, and enter into clinical relationships as individual practitioners. They and they alone are *finally* responsible for the quality of the services they provide and for the ethical context in which they are provided.

As professionals, clinicians are responsible for the consequences of their acts and must make every effort to ensure that their services are used appropriately and in the best interests of their clients.

Competence

As we noted earlier, the perception of professional expertise or competence is the cornerstone on which any profession rests. In terms of clinical practice in counseling, the ethical principles and issues involving competence are particularly crucial. Since human services professionals are prepared in a variety of ways and at several academic levels, the public may experience considerable confusion in understanding the scope and level of competence of any individual counselor.

The ethical clinician must, therefore, be especially scrupulous in observing the following injunctions.

Representation of Competence. Counselors must accurately represent their competence, education, training, and experience to clients or potential clients at all times. They should claim as evidence of professional competence only degrees or certificates earned from generally recognized and accredited institutions that are accepted by professional associations and other duly constituted groups as fully legitimate.

Each professional practitioner is responsible for correcting or clarifying any confusion or misapprehension about his or her credentials or qualifications on the part of any client or potential client. The failure to correct unrealistic perceptions of competence or qualifications is just as unethical as is a conscious deception.

Maintenance of Competence. Competence is, obviously, a changing and dynamic concept. Clinicians are ethically obligated to renew and extend their professional competence through continuing educational experiences. These are often formal experiences provided in the context of continuing education courses, workshops, seminars, or conferences. Very often these are sponsored or accredited by professional associations as part of their effort to enhance the growth of the profession.

Continuing education is not limited, however, to enrollment in special courses or programs. One basic expectation involved in the issue of competence is that counselors continue throughout their careers to read the professional literature, understand current developments in research, and attend to the changes in theory and practice that inevitably occur. In this sense the ever-changing nature of scientific knowledge makes it totally unrealistic to construe competence in any fixed or static sense.

A professional's level or scope of competence on the day of graduation from a preparation program is steadily eroded from that day forward unless that professional accepts the responsibility for maintaining such competence in a systematic way, using a variety of resources.

Defining the Scope of Individual Competence. Perhaps the most difficult and compelling issue for counselors that relates to the issue of professional competence involves defining the scope of one's own competence in relation to the needs of particular types or groups of clients. The range of needs and characteristics of people who may present themselves or be referred to any given practitioner is, of course, tremendous.

Clients may vary widely in terms of the nature and seriousness of psychological problems. They obviously vary in terms of characteristics such as age, sex, socioeconomic status, racial or ethnic membership, religious backgrounds, and many other variables that may influence the nature or course of treatment.

Counselors are confronted with the ethical problem of determining whether their own level and scope of professional competence warrants them to undertake a particular case.

The issue is complex and difficult. Most clinicians, quite properly, respond to any appeal for help from a prospective client with a sincere desire to provide assistance. Unfortunately, in many clinical situations the counselor's desire to help is not automatically equitable with having the professional expertise or competence genuinely *to be of help*. We know only too well that inexpert counseling may be worse than no counseling at all (Bergin, 1963).

Counselors must set clear and realistic boundaries around their

own areas of professional competence based on careful consideration of their own preparation and experience. These boundaries are
defined by the nature and severity of a client's presenting problems
and by the client's special characteristics. The professional judgments involved in setting and maintaining such boundaries are
difficult. In general, clinicians may safely take the conservative view
that professional competence to undertake clinical work with a
given client presenting a particular type of problem or set of characteristics is best attested to by successful *supervised* practice with
similar clients.

Similarly, when clinicians wish to extend their boundaries of
professional competence to work with new types of clients or to
utilize new approaches and techniques, they should seek supervised
clinical experience under the direction of experienced and well-
qualified clinicians having the desired competence.

In general, simply reading a book or attending a lecture on a given
topic is not sufficient to extend one's professional competence into a
new area of practice.

The Counselor's Level of Functioning. A final but very important
aspect of the issue of professional competence relates to the counsel-
or's own level of personal and psychological functioning. Counselors
are, after all, simply human beings subject to all of the same foibles
and frailties that beset other human beings. As such, counselors are
just as finite, limited, and imperfect as are those who seek them out
for help.

When counselors are beset by personal problems and concerns,
or suffer from excessive stress or fatigue, or incur any kind of illness, their ability or competence to help a given client may be
impaired. Even though such an impairment may be temporary
from the standpoint of the counselor, it may be crucial in the
life of a client.

Counselors have two major ethical obligations in this kind of
situation. First, they have an ethical obligation to recognize and to
act to protect clients when factors in their own lives disrupt, even
temporarily, their ability to provide quality services. Such actions
may involve referral to another counselor, or where the best interests of the client permit, a recess in a series of sessions.

The second ethical obligation of professional clinicians in this
area involves making every effort to organize and manage one's
personal life and professional practice in ways that prevent, where
possible, disruptions of professional competence. This obligation
involves assessing workloads realistically and so avoiding continual

overloads that may produce excessive fatigue or chronic stress reactions. It also involves the cultivation of good health habits in terms of diet, exercise, sleep, and recreation. Finally, it involves the development of self-awareness and the identification of one's own tolerance limits in terms of emotional and physical responses to stress.

The ethical counselor is not a "workaholic" to whom "commitment" or "dedication" is simply a way of rationalizing a driven, compulsive, and totally unexamined life-style. Such a personal style usually translates into a professional pattern in which the counselor drowns his or her own personal needs and problems in an unhealthy and often unhelpful overinvolvement with clients.

Moral and Legal Standards

Counselors are citizens for whom questions of legal and moral behavior pose the same kinds of issues that confront all members of a democratic and pluralistic society.

In some situations, however, counselors must be aware of how their behavior affects the public trust and confidence on which the profession is based. Ethical and professionally concerned counselors do not casually or flippantly disregard or ignore prevailing community standards for behavior. When, for good reason, they choose to behave in ways that may be perceived as unconventional or nonconforming, they are sensitive to the impact that such behavior may have on others and on the profession. Where appropriate, they articulate their convictions and value commitments clearly and publicly.

Ethical counselors are, of course, particularly sensitive to the legal and civil rights of clients. They do not behave in ways that will restrict or diminish those rights. Not infrequently clinicians are involved in situations in which they work with clients who are incarcerated, committed to hospitals by court order, or made wards of a court. In such situations counselors must be fully aware of the legal position and rights of all concerned. In some situations individuals have a right to refuse treatment or to refuse to participate in psychological assessment procedures.

Frequently counselors are involved in legal proceedings as witnesses. Often such litigation may involve questions of child custody or foster home placements. In such situations they should scrupulously adhere to legal procedures designed to ensure fairness and justice. When a clinician is called on to testify as an "expert," such testimony should be given carefully and in the context of the best scientific knowledge available.

Counselors should also be especially sensitive to situations in which clients or others are subjected to prejudice or unfair treatment because of racial, sexual, religious, or age bias. Clinicians cannot ethically condone or ignore such situations.

One of the most difficult ethical situations in this area of moral and legal issues arises when the counselor finds that immoral or illegal actions toward clients are occurring within the agency or institution of which the clinician is a part. Sometimes such action is actually the result of policies or procedures within the organization. Occasionally it may be the result of the attitudes or behaviors of members of the organization, including those who are in authority.

These situations are obviously very difficult for the ethical counselor. Although the practical circumstances may be very difficult, the nature of the ethical responsibilities involved is quite clear. Professional counselors cannot ethically ignore or condone unethical, immoral, or illegal behavior against clients or co-workers simply because such behavior is ignored, condoned, or perpetrated by those in authority in an employing agency. The professional counselor cannot delegate his or her ethical responsibilities to others.

In some cases the ethical clinician may have to be a "whistle blower," who calls attention to and demands action on unprofessional situations. In settings where such situations cannot be remedied, the counselor may have to seek employment elsewhere.

Advertising and Other Public Statements

In the course of professional practice, counselors and organizations employing counselors frequently make public announcements or statements designed to promote services or perhaps merely to inform the public about the nature of their services. Counselors are ethically obligated to ensure that such statements are accurate and objective and that they do not misrepresent the effectiveness of services provided. Statements made about professional services should reflect current scientific knowledge and should include full recognition of the limitations or uncertainties attached to such knowledge.

In making promotional statements about services, counselors should be especially careful not to confuse prospective clients. Promotional statements should not mislead or deceive by making only partial disclosures of facts. Such statements, of course, must not contain false or fraudulent claims. It is unethical to use testimonials from former clients, or to imply that professional services provided are unusual or unique or have mysterious or special properties. Statements should not create unjustified expectations of probable results. Similarly, it is unethical to play on the fears, anxieties, or apprehensions of prospective clients in order to induce them to seek professional help.

Finally, it is unethical to make direct comparisons of the relative desirability of competing services or agencies. Direct solicitation of individual clients is also unethical.

Many of the ethical constraints described above are most applicable to private practice situations or those in which counseling services are offered on a "for profit" basis. Increasingly, some kinds of counseling services are offered by private corporations. We should note that the ethical constraints described above apply whether professional counselors issue the public statements directly or such statements are issued by an employing organization, advertising agency, or other group.

It is unethical to offer inducements to media representatives to obtain publicity, and it is also unethical for counselors to accept fees or favors for giving testimonials on behalf of products or services.

Even in situations where counseling services are offered on a nonprofit basis in community or campus agencies, possibilities for misrepresentation still exist. When special programs such as growth groups or human relations training courses are given, for example, counseling centers, clinics, or other sponsoring agencies should give a clear and complete statement of the purpose of the program, the nature of the experiences provided, and the qualifications of the professionals providing leadership. When services are offered to the public for research or training purposes, the nature of those purposes and the impact on clients should be fully and unambiguously disclosed.

Statements in Media Presentations. Statements made in catalogs, brochures, or other materials should be accurate, current, and comprehensive. When counselors speak to the public through lectures, seminars, or conferences about professional ideas, problems, or issues, their statements should be based on accepted scientific knowledge; and where the presentation involves personal preferences, options, or points of view not based on factual evidence, the opinions expressed should be identified as such.

One very dubious development in recent years has been the

appearance of numerous radio and television programs that purport to offer counseling or quasi-counseling services directly in interviews conducted in a studio or to individuals who call in to the "counselor." Ethical codes such as those of the American Psychological Association (APA) and the American Association for Counseling and Development (AACD) clearly provide that counseling or therapeutic services should be provided within the context of professional psychological relationships. Strangely enough, current ethical codes do not speak explicitly enough to these media situations to specify clearly that they are unethical. In the opinion of the authors, however, any such media programming that purports to provide real services to actual clients in the context of providing a spectacle for public edification or amusement is of a very unsavory character and can only bring the profession into eventual disrepute.

Confidentiality

An ethical issue of primary importance to counselors is that of confidentiality. More practical ethical problems in clinical work arise out of questions of confidentiality than from any other issue. Many of these problems arise from the fact that counseling and psychotherapy always occur within a social context that involves both clinicians and clients in a network of interpersonal relationships.

Counselors and the agencies and organizations of which they are a part function within a larger community and relate to a variety of institutions and groups within that community. For community agencies to perform their functions optimally, some exchange of information is obviously desirable. That exchange, however, is always limited by the ethical imperative to respect the privacy, dignity, and desires of individual clients.

Similarly, clients also live within a social milieu reflecting a network of interpersonal relationships. In many counseling situations that network is an essential framework that supports the psychological functioning and the material and emotional well-being of the client. Here, too, some degree of communication among counselor, client, and client support systems again appears very desirable. Even in this context, however, the rights of the individual client to privacy are paramount.

Ethical obligations for confidentiality are, however, always relative rather than absolute. The right of an individual to have a confidence respected always exists within a context of other rights and values.

Professionals have always recognized the fact that the sanctity of human life outweighs the significance of a promise to keep a client's confidence. No counselor, for example, would be expected to maintain a confidence in which a client reveals that he has just placed a time bomb in a crowded auditorium.

Indeed, some courts (Paul, 1977) have held that in certain circumstances a counselor or therapist has a duty to warn an intended victim of a threat made on his or her life by a client.

At the same time, however, society has also clearly recognized that some kinds of professional relationships are so important to the welfare of individuals and ultimately, therefore, to society that they should not be intruded upon even in courts of law.

The principle of "privileged communication" protects the confidential nature of some special relationships. Essentially, a privileged relationship is one in which one member cannot be compelled to testify against another member in a criminal proceeding. Unfortunately, privileged communication usually tends to be restricted to attorney–client, physician–patient, and minister–parishioner relationships. In some states, however, communications with psychologists are also considered privileged. Privileged communication does not generally apply to all counselors, at least partially because the title of counselor is so difficult to define.

Confidentiality is, then, a very complex issue. Perhaps the simplest way to examine the issues involved is in terms of *levels of confidentiality*. We can specify three basic levels of confidentiality that can apply in any given clinical situation.

Level 1. The first and perhaps most frequently violated level of confidentiality involves simply the professional handling of all information that arises out of *any* professional situation or relationship. In professional situation we include all kinds of professional counseling services, including group work, consultations, training, or work with organizations.

At this level the basic imperative is that all information be handled in a fully professional manner that *respects the dignity, privacy, and worth* of all individuals and organizations involved. This kind of confidentiality applies not only to designated clients but to any other individuals or organizations, such as friends, family, schools, welfare agencies, and the like, about whom information may be obtained as part of the clinical process.

Professional handling of counseling information means that it will never be divulged in a careless, casual, or irresponsible way. Such information is never discussed in social conversation, never revealed in response to casual inquiries, and never used to enhance the ego or prestige of the professional involved.

This kind of confidentiality embraces *all* information about counseling contacts. Even the fact that a given individual has sought counseling or has been referred is treated as confidential.

Where records are kept of clinical interviews, telephone calls, appointments, and so forth, these should always be kept in locked files accessible only to professionals or other trusted employees.

Clerical workers who type or file materials should be carefully selected and thoroughly trained to respect this kind of confidentiality. Interview notes, open case files, or memoranda regarding clients should never be left unattended on desks or in typewriters. File drawers and desks should be routinely locked. Telephone inquiries about clients should be politely but firmly refused.

The kind of confidentiality described above should, of course, apply to all professionals in every situation. It represents a kind of fundamental concern and respect for people that is at the foundation of all professional relationships.

Level 2. A second level of confidentiality arises in almost every clinical situation. This level goes beyond the simple matter of handling information in responsible and professional ways. The defining feature of this level of confidentiality is that information will be used or divulged only *in the best interests of the client.*

One of the realities of clinical practice is that in many situations clients are referred from one professional to another for testing or special services. Many times clients are referred out to other agencies, or such agencies are consulted in regard to a given case. In many such situations information about clients is shared among professionals or agencies.

This kind of sharing of information is deemed to be in the best interest of the client and indeed is often necessary to bring the optimal set of resources to bear on the client's problems.

Many times counseling information is shared in this way not only between counselors but also with spouses, parents, teachers, or other people significant to the client. Counseling with children often produces situations in which sharing of information with parents is an essential part of treatment. Increasingly, treatment for adults for a variety of problems such as alcohol or drug abuse centers around the involvement of family members.

This kind of information sharing should always be done only in the best interest of the client and with the client's full knowledge.

When the client gives consent to this sort of sharing of information, obviously no ethical problems arise. When a client is reluctant or unwilling to have such information shared, very difficult problems may arise. Such problems may be avoided when the counselor carefully structures *in advance* with the client the counselor's or agency's policy in regard to sharing of information in the client's best interests.

When the counselor's or agency's policy in regard to information sharing is clear to the client *in advance*, many problems of sharing of information simply become matters of clinical judgment rather than ethical dilemmas.

A number of clinical situations may pose real difficulties for counselors at this level of confidentiality even when policies are clearly articulated, however. In some situations in which counselors work with minor children, serious problems arise when the legal custody of such children is disputed or unclear. Special policies in regard to the rights of noncustodial parents to obtain information may be required. In such situations the best interests of the child as well as the rights of parents must be considered.

Frequently, counselors accept referrals in which the costs of treatment are borne by someone other than the identified client. Parents, spouses, ex-spouses, employers, insurance companies, and others may at times pay for treatment. Often such payers feel that they have a right to obtain information or even to influence the course of counseling simply because they pay for that treatment.

Clearly, the simple fact that a particular individual or organization pays for clinical services does *not* convey to them any right of access to confidential information. Information should be made available only at the client's request and when it is in the client's best interest. Again, structuring policies on confidentiality clearly in advance in such cases may avoid misunderstanding.

Interestingly, the principle that information may be shared only in the client's best interests may preclude sharing information with certain individuals even when such release of information is requested by the client.

Counselors might ethically refuse to share information about a former client with clearly unethical or unqualified practitioners or "quacks" even though such releases are requested by the client. Certain kinds of information, such as results of projective personality devices, might be withheld if the counselor felt that the requesting practitioner was not qualified to interpret them appropriately.

Sometimes difficulties arise within an institution or agency when administrators or others seek information about a client who may be involved in disciplinary, academic, or legal difficulties. Again, administrative authority in itself does not convey an *ethical right* to obtain information. The counselor is ethically bound to serve the best interests of the client in handling information. Ethical principles and policies should be clearly understood within an agency, school, or other organization in advance of difficult situations.

Level 3. The third level of confidentiality goes beyond the other two in providing that *any* information divulged by a client in the course of the counseling relationship will be kept in complete confidence except in the most extreme condition such as a clear and imminent danger to human life. At this level of confidentiality the counselor is not free to share such information even though it may be viewed as desirable in terms of the client's best interests to do so. Similarly, administrative convenience, interagency relationships, and even the client's own family relationships do not justify divulging information without the express consent of the client.

When counselors operate at this highest level of confidentiality, they do so in the knowledge that many clients would not be willing to divulge psychologically significant information without this kind of commitment to confidentiality. The counselor contributes to the well-being of the client, and ultimately to the society, by providing a secure and psychologically close relationship in which a client can feel free to discuss deeply private and perhaps troubling thoughts and feelings.

At times receiving such confidences may be upsetting to the counselor. Keeping confidences and trusting in his or her own skills and knowledge to help a client work through very disturbing situations is often an ultimate test of the personal security and professional integrity of a counselor.

Clinicians who structure their professional relationships at Level 3 should not do so lightly. When the counselor leads a client to expect that this level of confidentiality will be extended, the resulting commitment constitutes a heavy responsibility.

Counselors who break confidences accepted at this level, except in situations where human life is at stake, are likely to cause psychological harm to their clients and will certainly bring themselves and their profession into disrepute. Counselors who break such confidences will soon have no confidences to keep.

As we have seen, the ethical issues surrounding confidentiality in clinical work are complex. Simple professionalism dictates, of course, that Level 1 be honored at all times. Counseling may be practiced ethically and professionally at either Level 2 or Level 3 as long as clients are made fully aware of the counselor's policy in advance. Clearly, the counselor who limits his or her commitments to Level 2 will be unable to work productively with some clients in some situations.

Counselors should be clear that once an ethical responsibility is undertaken, being *ordered* to break a confidence or to behave unethically is not an acceptable justification. In some extreme situations counselors may have to leave certain settings in order to maintain their ethical integrity.

Legal Aspects of Confidentiality. As we noted earlier, certain professional relationships are viewed as privileged and cannot be intruded on by the courts. Since most counseling situations are not viewed as privileged, counselors should be fully aware of their legal status. In most cases any kind of official record can be subpoenaed and placed in evidence in a court of law.

This means that in most situations counseling interview notes, case summaries, diagnostic reports, and so forth, when made part of a formal file or record, can be subpoenaed. Counselors should be acutely aware when they write such notes or reports that they are not completely private, at least insofar as the courts are concerned. Counselors should refrain from entering speculative conjectures or remarks into case notes or summaries and should be very cautious in assigning labels involving diagnostic categories to clients. Casual notations that a client seemed "paranoid" or "hostile" or even "disturbed" may be interpreted in very different ways at some later time.

When counselors wish to maintain privacy in their interview notes or other case materials, they must clearly address them as "memoranda to myself." Such memoranda must be kept exclusively in the counselor's possession, inaccessible to supervisors or clerical personnel, or they are likely to be viewed as a formal record. Such memoranda are not generally subject to subpoena, although the counselor may be ordered by a court to testify about their contents.

Since counseling relationships are usually not seen as privileged by the courts, counselors may be put in agonizing ethical dilemmas when ordered to testify about clients or former clients. When called to testify in court cases, counselors may wish to consult with their own attorneys regarding their legal rights and responsibilities. They may also wish to consult with their professional associations. In some situations professional associations may even provide legal assistance to professionals placed in difficult ethical situations by litigation involving clients.

The Welfare of Clients

Counseling services exist for the benefit of clients. The overriding value in almost any counseling situation is the ultimate welfare of the client. Individuals seeking counseling services have every right to expect that their welfare rests securely at the top of the counselor's value hierarchy.

Obviously, there are some limits around even this generalization. While the counselor frequently acts as the agent or advocate of the client, at times the counselor's obligations to the society and the profession might limit his or her willingness to provide services. Clearly, an ethical counselor, for example, would not help a client to feign a mental illness in order to defraud an insurance company or employer, or help a client to plan or carry out some other kind of criminal activity.

Within such professional limits, however, the client has a right to expect that the counselor will be able and willing to act on the client's behalf without any qualifications that may arise out of other interests or commitments.

Conflicts of interest, then, arise out of circumstances in which the counselor may have, or appear to have, commitments, self-interests, relationships, or investments that compete or conflict with the responsibilities undertaken on behalf of the client.

In order to avoid either the reality or appearance of conflicts of interest, counselors avoid entering into counseling relationships with individuals with whom they have close social, familial, or financial relationships.

In practice this means that counselors would not engage in counseling with family members or close friends or relatives. Similarly, they would not counsel with employees whom they supervise directly or with their own employers or supervisors. Counselors would also not enter into significant financial transactions with clients or their immediate families.

One of the most significant areas of potential conflicts of interest is the area of sexual relationships. Clearly, *any sexual relationship with a client is unethical.* There are no ethically valid exceptions to this principle. The sexual exploitation of clients in psychotherapy is, unfortunately, a well-documented phenomenon (Holroyd & Brodsky, 1977). It has only served to bring the helping professionals into disrepute and to harm or alarm many clients or potential clients.

One important factor that must be recognized in avoiding conflicts of interest in any area is that counseling relationships are not "symmetrical." That is, counseling relationships almost by definition place the counselor in a position of great social influence. Both the professional status of the counselor on entry into the relationship and the dynamics of the counseling process itself serve to enhance the power of the counselor and to place an already troubled client in a position of even greater vulnerability.

Ethical counselors must recognize and respect this vulnerability and refrain from behaving in any way that may exploit it. Sexual relationships with clients clearly represent an unethical exploitation of such possible vulnerability. Another related aspect of client vulnerability is sexual harassment. Sexual harassment may be defined as any unwanted attention or conversation of a sexual nature forced on someone in a subordinate or vulnerable situation by someone in a position of status or authority. Remarks, gestures, "off-color" jokes, or unwanted touching can all be interpreted as sexual harassment.

Conduct by a professional toward a client that may be interpreted as sexual harassment is unethical and unprofessional, and it serves to bring both the counselor and the profession into disrepute.

Counselors also safeguard the welfare of clients by terminating treatment when it is clear that the client is no longer benefiting from that counseling. Clients whom a counselor is no longer able to help but who desire further services may be referred for alternative kinds of assistance. Counselors do not accept remuneration for referring to another practitioner. Clients should also be given the widest range of choice practical in choosing a referral source.

When clients pay fees for services, the amount and basis for those fees should be discussed fully with them in advance. Questions of eligibility for third-party payments or arrangements for deferred payments should also be discussed fully. Ordinarily, clients in the midst of treatment or those who are in a vulnerable situation as a result of the progress of treatment should not be prematurely terminated because of the termination of insurance coverage or other inability to pay immediately.

Professional Relationships

Counselors frequently work closely with members of other helping professions. Indeed, utilizing the special skills and expertise of such professionals may be essential in providing an optimal combination of services for particular clients.

Counselors show respect and consideration in dealing with other professionals. They communicate with other professionals about clients within the limits of confidentiality discussed earlier.

Sometimes clinicians find that a client is receiving similar services from another professional. Counselors cannot ethically engage in such a duplication of services, which may be therapeutically counterproductive. When counselors learn that a client is being seen by another helping professional, the counselor should insist on contacting that professional to ensure that continuing his or her own relationship with the client is appropriate. The clinician should then discuss the continuation of services with the client.

Counselors who supervise other clinicians or helping professionals are obligated to help facilitate the professional growth of such individuals. They are responsible for helping to provide appropriate working conditions, thoughtful and timely evaluations, constructive consultation, and in-service learning experiences. Ethical counselors do not engage in sexual harassment or other exploitive or demeaning behavior with supervisees or employees.

Perhaps the most difficult ethical issue in the area of professional relationships is the problem involved when a counselor observes unethical or unprofessional behavior on the part of another professional. Clearly, the responsibilities of professional membership dictate that one counselor cannot condone or ignore unethical behavior on the part of another.

Minor ethical lapses may many times be due to thoughtlessness or ignorance. The counselor should first discuss the problem in a tactful but candid way with the counselor in question. If this approach is not successful and the unethical behavior continues or is not rectified, the counselor witnessing the situation is obligated to report the matter to those in authority in the organization. If this procedure fails, the counselor may have to report the problem to the appropriate professional association or to a public agency such as a licensing board.

The principle is clear that ignoring or condoning unethical behavior *is* unethical behavior.

STANDARDS FOR PROFESSIONAL PRACTICE

The ethical principles that we have just discussed deal primarily with specific aspects of professional relationships. We have discussed these principles primarily as they relate to counseling practice. Other aspects of these principles in relation to teaching, publication, and other aspects of professional life were not discussed in this chapter.

One important area of professional practice goes beyond specific aspects of the counselor–client relationship to examine the general context within which services are provided. These issues can be combined under the rubric of standards for professional practice.

In a very real sense, failure to maintain acceptable standards for professional practice is a betrayal of the general public trust and, more particularly, a betrayal of the profession itself. Because the profession has such a large stake in the maintenance of professional standards, professional associations take pains to promulgate and publicize such formal standards so that practicing professionals are fully aware of their obligations and responsibilities.

The APA (1977) has published statements on professional standards that apply both to the delivery of general psychological services and specifically to counseling psychology practice (see Appendix C). Not all counselors are counseling psychologists, of course, and some of the APA standards deal with definitions and injunctions that apply only to psychologists. Many of the standards, however, are equally relevant to all professional counselors and all settings in which counseling services are delivered. These standards were briefly outlined earlier in this book.

We will discuss and interpret below some of these broadly applicable standards in terms of their specific implications for practice:

1. *Standards for staffing counseling services.* Professional counselors are expected to limit their practice to their areas of professional competence. They are expected to maintain current knowledge of scientific and professional developments in their field and to continue to enhance their professional competence. They are encouraged to develop new and innovative programs and approaches. We discussed many of these considerations earlier.

2. *Organization of counseling programs.* Programs should be responsive to the needs of the clientele being served. In counseling agencies or organizations descriptions of the lines of responsibility,

roles, and functions of service providers and other aspects of the organizational structure should be available to consumers or to agencies that sanction or regulate such services.

This requirement means essentially that organizations that provide counseling services must be structured so that professional responsibilities involved in the delivery of such services can be readily recognized. Clients or others who may be dissatisfied with aspects of those services should be able to pinpoint responsibility. Written statements regarding the purposes and goals of service providers should also be available.

3. *Commitments of counseling service providers.* All providers of counseling services should be committed to support the legal and civil rights of clients. All providers should be committed to conform to the relevant laws and regulations established by federal, state, and local governments. All service providers should be committed to abide by the ethical codes and principles established by appropriate professional associations.

In essence, this standard means that counselors and counseling agencies operate within the ethical and legal frameworks established by the society. They accept regulation by government and monitoring by professional associations. The delivery of counseling services is thus clearly seen as an activity that is regulated and sanctioned in the public interest.

4. *Professional involvements of counselors.* Professional counselors should be fully involved in setting goals, formulating plans and strategies for delivering services, and assessing outcomes of services provided. They should serve on appropriate professional committees and have a voice in all decisions affecting the quality of services provided. They are responsible for monitoring the professionalism with which services are delivered.

Counselors are professionals, not merely employees of an agency or institution. As professionals, counselors share responsibility for all aspects of service delivery that bear on the well-being of clients. Counselors cannot function ethically and professionally in settings where authoritarian administrative policies or practices deny them the opportunity to function as full professionals.

5. *Maintenance of professional records and procedures.* Counseling service providers should have formal, written statements that define policies and practices that relate to such matters as screening of prospective clients, referral procedures, confidentiality, fee structures, third-party payments, handling of files and rec-

ords, and so forth. These policies and procedures should be available on request to users or sanctioners of counseling services.

The maintenance and storage of counseling case notes, records, assessment data, case summaries, and reports should be accomplished in a professional manner with attention to safeguarding the confidentiality of such materials. Arrangements for the privacy of clients in interview or assessment situations should also be ensured.

Essentially, this requirement means that counseling services must be provided within a formal, professional setting and situation. It is clearly unprofessional and unethical to attempt to provide such services in a careless, casual, or impromptu manner no matter how well-intentioned are the motives of the providers.

6. *Adequacy of counseling resources and services.* Counseling services should be provided and resources made available at a level adequate to meet the purposes of the program and the needs of clientele accepted. Adequate time for appointments should be provided, and appointments should be kept except in genuine emergency situations. Counseling loads of staff should be reasonable in terms of providing quality services. Where clients are accepted who have special needs or characteristics, such as ethnic or minority backgrounds, counselors should be available who have appropriate training and experience. Similarly, appropriate assessment tools, informational resources, and clerical support should be provided.

7. *Relationships to other services.* Counseling services should utilize and function as part of the full network of human services available in the community. Policies for cooperation, referral, and sharing of resources and information should be implemented within the limits of ethical obligations to clients.

8. *Accountability for quality of services.* Counseling service providers should accept their accountability to clients, the community, and the profession. Regular and systematic evaluation of the outcomes of specific cases and programs of services and of the adequacy of policies and procedures should be undertaken. Information about the outcomes of services and programs should be incorporated into planning activities to ensure constant improvement in the quality of services offered.

In the following chapter we will discuss ethical issues involved in psychological assessment practices and research activities. These two issues are discussed separately because they may occur either within or without counseling service delivery situations and settings.

REFERENCES

American Psychological Association. (1977). Standards for providers of psychological services. *American Psychologist, 32,* 495–505.
American Psychological Association. (1981). Ethical principles for psychologists. *American Psychologist, 36,* 635–638.
Bergin, A. E. (1963). The effects of psychotherapy: Negative effects revisited. *The Journal of Counseling Psychology, 10,* 244–249.
Bok, S. (1979). *Lying: Moral choice in public and private life.* New York: Vintage Books.
Holroyd, J., & Brodsky, A. (1977). Psychologists' attitudes and practices concerning erotic and nonerotic physical contacts with patients. *American Psychologist, 32,* 843–849.
Paul, R. E. (1977). Tarasoff and the duty to warn: Towards a standard of conduct that balances the rights of clients against the rights of third parties. *Professional Psychology, 8,* 126–128.

Chapter Six
Ethical Issues in Assessment and Research

For many years the area of psychological assessment has been fraught with controversy and acrimonious debate. In particular the usefulness, fairness, and social value of psychological tests and inventories has been questioned and argued, often with more vehemence than good sense.

In a very broad sense the assessment process is a pervasive and virtually inevitable aspect of almost any kind of psychological activity. To the degree that counselors try to understand their clients, some sort of assessment activity is almost certainly a part of any helping process.

Within a counseling relationship, assessment activities are primarily intended to facilitate the helping process, that is, to assist the counselor in his or her effort to work successfully with the client around the client's own set of goals, needs, and aspirations.

Counselors use a wide range of techniques and instruments in assessing, that is, in coming to understand the client more fully. In this sense the counseling interview itself is a kind of discovery process that helps the counselor to unearth and organize significant information about the client. Often the counselor also employs other devices such as various questionnaires, inventories, and psychological tests as part of the assessment process.

It is interesting to note that most of the controversy in assessment centers around these formal assessment tools and tends largely to ignore their role in the larger process of psychological assessment.

In many of these controversies it almost appears that some people see psychological tests and inventories as a kind of devil to be cast out. In this sense such people tend to focus on inanimate objects as sources of evil or unhappiness rather than on the significant usage of those objects, which is really at the root of human difficulties or problems.

Psychological tests are not at the root of problems of unprofessional or antisocial aspects of assessment any more than "demon rum" is responsible for alcoholism. Questionnaires, inventories, and tests are inanimate, ethically neutral, human inventions. They are neither good nor bad in themselves, but like all human inventions they can be used and misused for a wide range of purposes to produce a great variety of consequences ranging from the noble to the nefarious.

Psychological assessment devices, including interviews, questionnaires, inventories, and tests, are merely ways of making observations of human behavior. Such devices, then, are ways of observing a sample of human behavior from which we infer other behavior.

ETHICAL ISSUES IN ASSESSMENT

The ethical issues that underlie psychological assessment are rooted in the overall process of observation and inference and the ways in which people act on those inferences. The use of psychological tests and other assessment devices raises difficult ethical issues, not merely because the tests themselves are not perfectly valid, totally reliable, or completely infallible. The real ethical issues and dangers lie in the fact that they are frequently misused by fallible human beings, or used on behalf of goals or purposes that may in themselves be unethical or asocial.

The Context of Assessment

When psychological assessment tools are used in the context of counseling relationships characterized by the ethical principles discussed in Chapter 5, they present relatively few additional ethical problems. Obviously, such assessment devices should be chosen, utilized, and interpreted in competent ways for the benefit of the client. Principles regarding confidentiality, conflict of interest, and professional competence apply in virtually the same ways to the use of assessment procedures as to any other aspect of the counseling relationship.

Most of the special ethical problems and issues surrounding the area of psychological assessment arise because assessment procedures are very frequently used in situations in which the individual being assessed is clearly not a client. A great many psychological assessment situations arise not out of counseling relationships in which there is a clearly identifiable "helper and helpee" but rather occur as part of selection or admission programs, judicial proceedings, or other quite complex social and organizational contexts.

The ethical principle regarding assessment techniques promulgated by the American Psychological Association (APA) (1981) states in its preamble that psychologists utilizing such techniques "make every effort to promote the welfare and best interests of the client" (p. 637). Unfortunately, many situations in which psychological assessment procedures are undertaken are such that it may not be at all clear that the person being assessed is *anybody's* client in a practical and meaningful sense of the term.

Who, for example, is the client of a psychologist doing a psychological assessment as part of a presentencing investigation for a court? Who is the client in a testing situation that is part of an admissions procedure for graduate or professional school? Who is the client in an assessment situation involving promotion and retention in an executive training program for a giant corporation? In all of these situations it seems quite clear that the assessment process is being used *on* individuals, rather than *for* the individuals being assessed.

When counselors or counseling psychologists engage in assessment situations that arise outside a clear-cut counseling or helping relationship with an identified client, the entire ethical context in which the assessment is accomplished must be considered. The ethical counselor can never divorce himself or herself from the context in which the assessment information will ultimately be used. Typically, assessment information is used to make decisions that impact on the lives of individual human beings. In an ethical sense the professional doing the assessment and the assessment process itself are inevitably part of the total decision-making process. Clearly, the ethical responsibilities involved are shared to some degree by *all* concerned.

Counselors should not, for example, engage in assessment activities that are used to support or justify unfair discrimination in employment, promotion, or educational opportunities that are based on race, sex, religion, ethnic origin, age, or other arbitrary characteristics. When counselors engage in assessment activities with individuals or groups that have frequently been targets of unfair discrimination practices, it is incumbent on the counselor to do everything possible to ensure that the overall assessment process is fair and unbiased, that appropriate inferences are drawn from the assessment results obtained, and that the decisions based on the assessment information are fair, objective, and unbiased.

Obviously, in many situations the injunction above is very difficult to follow. In the APA *Ethical Principles for Psychologists* (1981) discussed above, the statement made merely says that psychologists "strive to ensure the appropriate use of assessment techniques by others" (p. 637). Many of the key ethical issues surrounding psychological assessment clearly rest on the *use* of the information obtained. When assessment data are used primarily to label people, to take troublesome students out of the educational mainstream, or to allow social institutions and agencies to "cop out" in terms of their responsibilities to provide fair opportunities and humane treatment, the ethical problems surrounding the entire assessment process are very real and very difficult to resolve.

Requirements for Ethical Assessments

Even though the counselor is unable, in a practical sense, to ensure totally the ethical use of information, several important safeguards are still possible and are ethically required. Several of these ethical imperatives are listed below:

1. In using assessment procedures counselors must respect the right of the individual being assessed to have a full and accurate explanation of the nature and purposes of the assessment procedure. This applies to all sorts of assessment procedures, not merely standardized tests. The only exception to this rule is when the subject has agreed to relinquish this right in advance. When a person other than the individual using the assessment technique gives such an explanation, the professional conducting the assessment is still responsible for ensuring the accuracy and adequacy of that information. Explanations should be given clearly in language that the subject can fully understand. The use of unfamiliar technical jargon to confuse or misinform the subject is clearly unethical.

2. When professionals report assessment results in any form, they are responsible for including in that report all of the limitations or reservations that exist regarding validity or reliability, circumstances around the assessment situations, appropriateness of norms for a given use, and any other relevant factors. Again, as we noted earlier, the professional strives to ensure that the information obtained is not misused.

3. Professionals recognize that assessment results may become obsolete, that is, they no longer reflect an accurate picture of the subject. Every effort should be made to prevent the misuse of obsolete information. This injunction may mean that counselors routinely discard obsolete assessment results, or make sure that reports and results are carefully dated, and that cautions about their timeliness are included in files or records.

4. Professionals do not encourage or promote the use of assessment techniques or data by untrained or unqualified people. When specific types of data are to be used by teachers, parents, or youth workers, for example, the professional accepts responsibility for training or supervising such people in the appropriate use of the techniques or information.

5. Perhaps the most important ethical imperative related to the use of assessment techniques is that the person being assessed has a *right to know the results*, the *interpretations* made, and the basis for the *conclusions* and *recommendations* made as a result of the assessment.

In some situations this means that the professional must communicate disturbing or distressing information to the client or subject. The professional is responsible for providing information in a clear, understandable way that is appropriate to the level of sophistication of the subject.

The individual's "right to know" is not limited to information arising out of counseling relationships. Psychological assessment results obtained in college admissions processes, routine educational testing, employment application processes, or hospital treatment may all be subject to the individual's right to know. In many situations this right extends to the parents or guardians of minor children on whom the information was obtained.

6. Professionals are responsible for developing, standardizing, scoring, or interpreting assessment devices and for following accepted scientific procedures. Standards for the development, publication, and use of psychological tests have been published by the APA (1974).

ETHICAL ISSUES IN RESEARCH

Both counselors and counseling psychologists frequently engage in research activity or practice in settings where research is done. When research activities utilize human subjects, ethical obligations designed to safeguard the welfare and interests of human subjects are incurred by researchers, organizations sponsoring research, and professionals working in research settings. In some kinds of research projects and settings, the issues that arise around these obligations may be quite complex.

In recent years the social and philosophical context in which research with human subjects is done has undergone dramatic changes. In traditional views of scientific research one fundamental assumption involved the clear dichotomy between the investigator or scientist and the phenomenon under investigation (Bergman, 1943). Research was done *on* a given phenomenon and a given set of subjects. Subjects were the organisms to be observed, studied, and manipulated in the interest of science and, of course, in the interest of the scientist.

As research with human subjects done around social and behavioral phenomena developed on a larger and larger scale, a number of fundamental questions was raised about the scientist–subject dichotomy. Some philosophers of science (Schrodinger, 1952) raised questions about whether it is possible to study social and behavioral phenomena in the same relatively detached and objective way in which science supposedly investigates other aspects of the natural world.

The philosophical questions raised about social and behavioral research centered on the issue of whether one human being can ever really detach himself or herself from social phenomena involving other human beings in the same way that a microbiologist studies the reproduction of microbes or a physicist studies the properties of subatomic particles. These kinds of questions have generated a great deal of discussion about the very nature of social and behavioral research. These difficult issues have certainly not been resolved, and in this book we are more concerned with the ethical and moral issues generated out of the philosophy of science than with the purely epistemological ones.

As researchers were confronted with the essential relationships between scientist and subject in a social or behavioral study, they also began to examine the ethical and moral questions involved. Even if scientists were *able* to study other human beings in fully impersonal, dispassionate, and objective ways, *should* they indeed do so?

Is it ethically acceptable to think of, or to treat, human beings purely as "subjects" to be observed, examined, manipulated, and constrained for the advancement of the science and for the edification of the scientist? These kinds of questions were made more compelling by the war crimes trials conducted at the end of World War II. The world learned to its horror that German and Japanese scientists had performed "experiments" on helpless human beings that exceeded in sheer cruelty and inhumanity anything that could be imagined by a writer of Hollywood horror movies.

As attention to abuses of human subjects was focused on research done in this country, the disturbing reality was made apparent that ethical problems around research were not solely confined to wartime savagery or brutal fascist regimes. Instances were widely reported of research projects in which sick human beings were left untreated, whole populations were exposed to bacterial infections, or participants were subjected to disturbing or humiliating deceptions.

Gradually, a new ethical framework for research was developed in which researchers and "subjects" were seen as *partners* and co-participants in a process of scientific inquiry, aimed at advancing human knowledge but also vitally concerned with protecting the welfare and dignity of all those concerned.

These new developments in thinking about the ethical obligations of researchers were articulated in what is called the Belmont Report of the National Commission for the Protection of Human Subjects of Biomedical and Behavioral Research (1979). This report became a primary basis for ethical standards in research and became part of the public policy framework that governed the award of research grants by the federal government.

Today the basic principles outlined in this report are generally accepted by most granting agencies, research institutions, and professional associations. They are also reflected in the ethical principles of the APA (1981).

Basic Principles for Ethical Research

The Belmont Report articulated a number of basic assumptions and principles around which to orient ethical approaches to research with human subjects. One basic assumption and several principles are discussed below.

The first general assumption articulated in the Belmont Report was the view that there must be clear and definite boundaries established between research and professional practice. Unless such boundaries exist, it will be impossible to identify and review research activities in terms of their potential impact on human subjects. Similarly, unless such boundaries exist, clients seeking professional services may be unaware that they are being "used" as subjects in a research program primarily designed and intended to generate new knowledge, rather than to deliver immediate services.

This distinction seems obvious and simple on the surface. In reality, however, particularly in fields such as counseling and psychotherapy, it may not be easy to apply. At times the distinction between research and practice may be blurred because both kinds of activities may occur together. Such a situation exists when, for example, treatment programs are being evaluated through the use of experimental designs. Indeed, the term "experimental" is often used loosely and often produces some confusion.

Generally speaking, the term "professional practice" refers to interventions that are designed *solely* to enhance the well-being of an individual client and that have a reasonable expectation of success. The purpose of professional practice is to provide needed services to identified clients.

The purpose of research is seen, on the other hand, to test hypotheses or draw conclusions and thereby contribute to a body of knowledge about some phenomenon. Obviously, there are times when research and practice go together, and indeed there are times when it is ethically incumbent on the practitioner to conduct research and evaluation to determine if a new treatment procedure is safe and effective.

When research and professional practice are carried on together, however, the combined program must be reviewed to consider its impact on participants in the same way as any other research project. The rule established in the Belmont Report is that if there is *any* component of research in an activity, that activity should be reviewed for the protection of the human subjects involved.

The Report defines three basic ethical principles that should govern the planning and review of research programs involving human subjects: respect for persons, beneficence, and justice.

Respect for Persons. This principle is obviously relevant to the discussion earlier about changes in the way research subjects are viewed. Respect for persons implies two basic considerations. First, it implies that all persons must be treated as *autonomous*, that is, having the right and ability to make choices regarding their own actions and commitments. The second aspect of this principle is that when for any reason the basic autonomy of individuals has been diminished they are entitled to *protection.*

Respect for human autonomy essentially involves acknowledging and accepting an individual's right and capacity to set his or her own personal goals and to act on them. Such respect involves giving attention and weight to another person's opinions and choices while refraining from obstructing his or her actions unless these are clearly detrimental to others.

When researchers ignore or repudiate a person's judgments, deny him or her the freedom to act on those considered judgments, or withhold or distort information necessary to make such judgments, those researchers have in effect refused to respect that individual's right to autonomy.

In some situations, including many kinds of psychological research, persons are encountered whose autonomy has clearly been diminished. Minor children, the emotionally disturbed or mentally retarded, patients committed to institutions, inmates of prisons, or even very seriously ill or handicapped people may, depending on the total set of circumstances, have diminished autonomy. That is, they may not be fully capable of self-determination either in the sense of making choices or in being free to act on them.

Respect for such persons may at times involve *protecting* them as they mature, recover, or are rehabilitated, or while they are incapacitated. Researchers and those who assist them are responsible for providing needed protection and, above all, for avoiding any exploitation of these persons' diminished autonomy or status.

This means practically that when researchers work in settings or institutions housing or serving persons with diminished autonomy, very special care must be taken to ensure their protection. We discuss the practical procedures involved in such circumstances under the heading "Obtaining Informed Consent."

Beneficence. The second basic ethical principle governing the planning and conduct of research with human subjects is termed *beneficence.* The principle of beneficence implies that people are treated in an ethical way, not only by respecting their decisions and protecting them from harm but also by making active efforts to ensure or enhance their well-being. The principle of beneficence is seen as an active obligation that involves the responsibility of the researcher both to maximize possible benefits to human subjects and to minimize possible harm.

The obligations involved in the principles of beneficence affect both individual researchers and society at large. The principle extends beyond individual research projects to the entire enterprise of scientific research. Again, we can see that the whole perspective within which contemporary scientific research is seen has shifted to one of a socially conscious and concerned set of activities that exists, at least in part, to enhance the public welfare.

When any kind of research enterprise involves any risk of harm to participants, that risk must be weighed in terms of the potential social and individual benefits that may ensue from it.

Obviously, the principle of beneficence, with its focus on potentials for benefit or harm to individuals, often involves very difficult choices. The point is that in the planning and conduct of research programs these kinds of concerns must always be considered.

Research projects that are totally frivolous, based on idle curiosity, or accomplished solely to enhance the status or enrich the purse of a researcher may be viewed as unethical to the degree that they may cause possible harm in the absence of any real social benefits.

Justice. The third basic operating principle involved in ethical research is the principle of justice. Essentially, the principle of justice deals with the question of who ought to receive the benefits of research and who ought to bear its burdens. In other words, the issue is one of fairness, or what is deserved. Injustices occur when some benefit to which a person is entitled is denied without good reason, or when some burden or disadvantage is imposed arbitrarily.

When either burdens or benefits accruing from a research program are distributed, the principle of justice demands that this distribution be based on some set of fair and reasonable criteria, such as the following: (a) to each person an equal share; (b) to each person according to individual need; (c) to each person according to individual effort; (d) to each person according to social contribution; or (e) to each person according to individual merit.

Questions of justice in connection with research ethics may at first seem strange or artificial. Usually these questions are associated with issues such as taxation, legal punishments, or economic rewards.

In fact, however, questions of justice are relevant to contemporary views of the social enterprise of scientific research. Should research involving risks, discomfort, inconvenience, or even boredom routinely be accomplished using subjects from what are essentially "captive" populations? In the past a very large proportion of medically oriented research, for example, has been done in public hospitals on patients who are unable to pay for other types of treatment. Vast amounts of psychological research have been done on undergraduate students, who of necessity become part of the ubiquitous "psychology subject pool." Much research has been done on prisoners, inmates of psychiatric hospitals, military personnel, the unemployed, and so forth. In all of these cases the burden of contributing to research efforts as a subject has tended to fall on those who are relatively powerless.

It is not coincidental that we have relatively few psychological studies of U.S. senators, presidents of major corporations, or navy admirals.

The principle of justice demands that we scrutinize the ways in which subjects are selected and the settings in which research is conducted to determine whether burdens are equitably distributed.

Similarly, the ways in which research problems are selected or how funding is supplied should be studied to ensure that the potential benefits of research activity are equitably distributed.

Applications of Ethical Principles in Research

The principles above are relatively abstract and often are not easy to apply. When they are applied in practical situations, the ensuing judgments are often difficult to make. We can, however, examine a set of procedural steps that can be taken to ensure that important ethical considerations are brought to bear on the development of any research project. Several of these steps are described below.

Assessment of Potential Risk or Harm. The first step in reviewing the ethical considerations involving human subjects deals with the assessment of risk. In assessing this factor, both physical and psychological risks must be considered. Similarly, both overt harm caused directly by some research procedure and harm caused by withholding or denying some helpful or positive resource must be considered. It is clearly the obligation of the researcher to *minimize* risk to human subjects in every way possible without impairing the value of the project. Where unavoidable levels of risk remain, these must be weighed against the potential social benefit of the research project.

Obtaining Informed Consent of Subjects. When researchers recruit subjects for a study, they must fully, accurately, and clearly inform potential subjects of all facts about the study that may affect the potential subject's willingness to participate. Potential risks to subjects are of course of special significance, but all other relevant factors that may influence the potential subject's decision must also be presented.

In some situations certain elements of deception within the study may be permissible where a final debriefing corrects the subject's understanding. Deceptions that may influence the subject's willingness to participate, however, are clearly *unethical*.

Obtaining informed consent in situations where potential subjects have diminished autonomy presents especially difficult problems. In such cases informed consent may have to be obtained from parents, guardians, courts, or other persons or agencies clearly responsible for protecting the welfare of the individuals involved. In situations where great social pressure may be brought to bear on potential subjects to participate, the researcher is responsible for preventing undue influence from operating. Sometimes this is done by withholding the identities of nonparticipants or refusers from those in positions of authority or influence.

The Right to Withdraw from the Research. In any research project, opportunity must be made available for any subject to withdraw at any time during the study. Such a decision to withdraw must be accepted by the researchers without attempts to use undue social influence or persuasion. When clients are paid or remunerated for participation, this does not relieve the researchers of any ethical obligations, including respecting the right to withdraw.

Respect for the Dignity and Privacy of Subjects. In any data collection or storage situation, the dignity and privacy of subjects must be respected. Generally, data sheets should bear identifying numbers rather than names. All identifying data should be stored in a secure place while needed, and destroyed when they no longer are required for the purposes of the study for which the subject gave informed consent. No other or further use of such data is permissible without additional consent. Research data obtained for special research projects under informed consent should not routinely be made part of the files or records of a sponsoring agency. Further contacts with subjects to ask permission for follow-up studies or for additional research should be made only by the original researchers or sponsoring agencies.

Debriefing of Subjects. Careful debriefing of all subjects should be accomplished to ascertain that no unforeseen harm or risk has been incurred. Where any deception or withholding of information has been part of a study, the debriefing process should remove such deception and remedy any possible confusion, misunderstanding, or tension induced by the study. Where appropriate, debriefing or follow-up contact should utilize the opportunity for the subject to learn or grow from the research experience. When information obtained from a subject indicates a possible need for some kind of professional service, such information should be interpreted to the subject and appropriate referrals offered.

Dissemination or Publication of Results. Any publication or other dissemination of research findings should ordinarily protect the identity of individual subjects and hosting agencies. This may be done by concealing and/or disguising the identity of subjects and by referring to times, places, and events in very general ways. Where case study data are reported, it is the responsibility of the researcher to disguise individual identities or to obtain explicit consent from subjects for any kind of publication.

As the reader will have noted by now, the ethical problems involved in protecting human subjects may be complex. Many universities and other research-oriented institutions or agencies maintain regular Human Subjects Research committees to review all relevant research proposals. Even where such committees review research projects, however, the final ethical responsibilities remain with the researchers.

Cross-Cultural Research and Research with Minorities

One other important set of ethical issues involving research activities should be mentioned. Frequently, researchers in the social and behavioral sciences conduct and publish research with populations of minority members. Almost by definition such groups may be disadvantaged economically or socially or may have a history of discrimination, bias, or persecution at the hands of more powerful groups. In many cases the proposed research activity may have a bearing on the problems or concerns of the minority group or may bear on issues of public policy that affect their status or welfare. Many times the issues involved are complex, controversial, and deeply emotional.

In these kinds of research settings and situations, researchers may be perceived as intrusive, meddlesome, or even as tools of oppressive forces or groups. Researchers need to be especially sensitive in such situations, both to the perceptions and feelings of subjects and potential subjects and to the ways in which research findings will be reported, published, and utilized.

In many cross-cultural research situations, researchers are well-advised to involve members of the group or community with which the research is concerned in very active roles in helping to plan, organize, conduct, and report the study. When such involvement is obtained early in the development of the project, many ethical difficulties may be avoided.

When research findings are published that may bear on emotionally charged or highly controversial topics or issues, it is especially important that such reports reflect all of the cautions, limitations, and uncertainties involved in interpreting the findings. In many such situations it may be useful to publish with such reports a set of rejoinders or reactions that reflect alternative interpretations or explanations of the study, particularly as these relate to controversial or social policy questions.

Free and open inquiry is an essential part of any democratic society. Freedom is inevitably accompanied, however, by personal and social responsibility.

ETHICAL ISSUES IN TRAINING

Many of the same ethical issues described above in connection with clinical research also bear on situations in which services are used to provide training for counselors-in-preparation. Prospective clients should be clearly informed of the nature of the training situation, the experience and qualifications of trainees providing services, and the nature of the supervision provided. Qualifications of supervisors, as well as the general legal and ethical framework within which both the training and services are provided, should be communicated. It is unethical to provide training by recruiting clients in any haphazard or ad hoc way. Generally, counseling agencies providing services for training purposes should adhere to the same general professional standards expected of other agencies.

When interviews or other counseling procedures are observed or recorded for training purposes, such observations can be made only with the informed consent of clients. Where clients may have diminished autonomy, the same procedures should be followed as in research. Recordings and interview or supervisory notes should be kept in secure places. Where cases are presented in training groups, such presentations should be covered by informed consent.

Case presentations outside the immediate training situation should adequately disguise the identity of an individual client or be covered under informed consent. Ordinarily tape recordings made for training purposes should be erased when they are no longer needed for the express purposes covered in the informed consent agreement. When counseling services are provided for training purposes, the professionals providing and supervising such services are ethically responsible for the quality of such services and their outcomes.

Ethical issues in assessment, research, and training are just as important and in some ways more complex than those encountered in regular clinical practice. In both kinds of situations unethical practice results in harm to individuals and to a breakdown in public trust and confidence. Professionals have the same obligations to report and to correct unethical practices in assessment, research, or training situations as they incur in regular clinical practice.

REFERENCES

American Psychological Association. (1974). *Standards for educational and psychological tests.* Washington, DC: Author.

American Psychological Association. (1981). Ethical principles for psychologists. *American Psychologist, 36,* 635–639.

American Psychological Association, American Educational Research Association, & National Council on Measurement in Education. (1974). *Standards for educational and psychological tests.* Washington, DC: American Psychological Association.

Bergmann, G. (1943). Outline of an empiricist philosophy of physics. *American Journal of Physics, 11,* 248–258.

The National Commission for the Protection of Human Subjects of Biomedical and Behavioral Research. (1979). *Ethical principles and guidelines for the protection of human subjects of research.* Washington, DC: Department of Health, Education, and Welfare.

Schrodinger, E. (1952). *Science and humanism.* London: Cambridge University Press.

III
Ethical Counseling: Cases and Methods of Analysis

In all of the laments and reproaches made by our seers and prophets, one misses any mention of "sin," a word which used to be a veritable watchword of prophets. It was a word once in everyone's mind, but now rarely if ever heard. Does that mean that no sin is involved in all our troubles—sin with an "I" in the middle? Is no one any longer guilty of anything? Guilty perhaps of a sin that could be repented and repaired or atoned for? Is it only that someone may be stupid or sick or criminal—or asleep? Wrong things are being done, we know; tares are being sown in the wheat field at night. But is no one responsible, no one answerable for these acts? Anxiety and depression we all acknowledge, and even vague guilt feelings; but has no one committed any sins?

Where, indeed, did sin go? What became of it?

—Karl Menninger, *Whatever Became of Sin?*

Chapter Seven
Examining Ethical Problems in Case Situations

In the preceding chapters of this book we have attempted to describe many of the ethical principles and issues that relate to the practice of counseling and counseling psychology. We have traced the philosophical roots of some of these issues and have endeavored to show how thinking about ethical questions and framing ethical decisions is a function of the total cognitive development of an individual counselor.

Above all, we have stressed that ethical problems and ethical principles are concerns of major import in terms of both the practice of individual counselors and the well-being of the profession itself. We have repeatedly pointed out that the practice of counseling is built on trust and that trust is based on confidence in the ethical integrity of the counselor and the profession.

If ethical issues and ethical principles are to have genuine impact on practice they must be applied to specific cases. It is one thing to read the ethical codes promulgated by the profession and quite another to face squarely the often agonizing dilemmas with which one is altogether too often confronted in clinical practice.

Earlier we discussed the four-step model of ethical behavior described by Rest (1984). It is worthwhile reviewing that model again as we endeavor to apply ethical principles to a variety of specific case situations. It provides a practical process model with which to conceptualize ethical problems.

FOUR-STEP MODEL OF ETHICAL BEHAVIOR

Step 1

Rest's first step is, of course, recognizing that an ethical problem exists. In this initial phase we must first recognize that our own behavior—that is, our own choices, decisions, and actions—will impact on the lives of others. In a sense this phase involves *ethical sensitivity*. Ethical sensitivity is essentially a form of empathy. When we are ethically sensitive, we can construe a complex situation from the perspective of others. We can "feel" the impact of our actions on their lives and begin to recognize that we are obligated to think carefully and to behave responsibly toward those others.

As we saw earlier, empathy, or perspective-taking, is heavily a function of our level of cognitive development. As we grow cognitively, we are increasingly able to empathize with or take into account the needs, viewpoints, and perspectives of others.

Counseling is a profession that both demands and invites us to grow cognitively throughout our preparation and our actual careers. Each new client, each new problem or tangled set of relationships that we encounter in clinical practice should move us toward greater and greater capacities for empathic understanding. As we travel this thorny path of professional development, we become more and more sensitive to ethical issues and concerns. Many times this increased sensitivity is disturbing and troubling as well as gratifying. In one sense our increased sensitivity deepens our sense of ethical responsibility and sharpens our awareness of the complexity of those ethical situations with which we must deal.

We realize all too well that clients come to us and to our colleagues precisely because they have confidence in our willingness to struggle responsibly with all of the complexities and ambiguities involved in the real-life situations of which they are a part.

Step 2

The second step in Rest's model flows inevitably from the sensitivity involved in the first. As we sense the impact of our behavior on others, we are forced to think logically and rationally about the probable consequences of our actions. In practice this process involves identifying some principle or set of principles that we can use to define our obligations and within which we can frame our choices.

These kinds of "first order" principles in a sense generate values with which we can make choices among the probable outcomes of alternative courses of action. We saw in Chapter 3 that philosophers and moralists have identified a number of overarching moral and ethical theories with which to view human events. We have listed a number of these in Table 7.1.

Although these great overarching first-order principles or theories provide the roots from which our ultimate ethical principles flow, they are necessarily quite abstract and often seem remote from the practical judgments with which we are confronted on a daily basis. We tend to bridge the gap between our abstract ethical theories and our practical judgments with a set of "second order" principles that offer more specific and concrete guides to action. It is these second-order principles that define our obligations and generate the value judgments that we can use to choose among the possible ethical alternatives available to us.

Steininger, Newell, and Garcia (1984) list 12 such second-order principles. Each principle defines a "good" or value to which we may feel committed and obligated. These principles are listed and described in Table 7.2.

In this second step, then, we draw on our set of second-order principles to define the outcomes or consequences that we intend to flow from our actions. Often we are forced to set priorities and choose between second-order principles when, as is often the case, more than one applies; yet the actions involved to implement them are incompatible.

Not surprisingly, when people act on the basis of different second-order principles, or rank-order them in different ways, their intended actions or ethical decisions *differ*. One of the most profound yet complicating facts about the whole realm of ethics is that two equally concerned and conscientious people, both acting on principles, can and frequently do disagree or act in different ways when confronted with the same ethical dilemma. To some extent, codes of ethics defined by the profession itself set limits around those disagreements by imposing certain kinds of professional priorities.

TABLE 7.1 General Moral Theories

1. Authority of God/conscience
2. Authority of duty/imperative
3. Laws of nature
4. Laws of happiness and pleasure
5. Human interests
6. Situational criteria

TABLE 7.2 Second-Order Principles

1. Veracity—telling the truth
2. Privacy—respecting other people and their property
3. Autonomy—respecting people's rights to determine their fates
4. Promise keeping—keeping promises
5. Parentalism—safeguarding the rights of those who cannot do so themselves
6. Self-improvement—improving ourselves
7. Nonmaleficence—doing no willful harm to others
8. Equality—generally treating everyone equally
9. Sanctity of life—believing all living things are intrinsically valuable

As we will soon see, however, even these ethical codes seldom *completely* define the preferred or ethical course of action. In almost every situation the final and often agonizing choice of principles, values, and outcomes is left to the individual counselor.

Step 3

Rest's third step involves developing a plan or strategy with which to implement the value decisions made and so secure the intended outcome. Often implementing ethical decisions involves considerable clinical skill and knowledge about human behavior.

Step 4

The final step in the whole process involves the "doing." Many times the actions involved require strength of character and firm resolve. Frequently, in the doing of ethical behavior we incur the wrath or disappointment of people whose respect and goodwill we value. Sometimes we incur real losses of both a material and a psychological nature as we adhere to our ethical decisions. We may lose a client, a friend, or even a job by being true to our principles. Ethical behavior often does not come without a price.

In the chapter that follows you will be presented with a number of practical case situations that generate difficult ethical problems. As you consider each try to use the Rest model.

As we apply this model, we are forced to ask and ultimately to answer the sequence of questions below:

1. How does the counselor's behavior impact on relevant others? Who? How? When? To what extent?

2. What are the second-order principles that apply to this situation? Which do I view as paramount or overriding in this situation?

3. What are the specific positive values that I would intend to maximize in this situation? What are the negatives that I would most wish to avoid?

4. What are the specific alternative courses of action open to me as a counselor in this situation? What are the probable consequences of each? For the counselor? For the client? For others?

5. How do these consequences compare in terms of the overriding principle that I have declared and the values that flow from that principle?

6. How can I develop a plan of action to implement my principles and values?

7. How can I act on these principles? What prices might I have to pay? How will my actions reflect on the profession and on my future practice?

It may be helpful before we begin our chapter of case presentations to illustrate the complex, multidimensional nature of ethical dilemmas in counseling. We will discuss in some detail one such practical case situation.

Several years ago a graduate student in a master's level program in counseling was assigned to a city high school for a counseling internship experience. During her first week in the school the intern was sitting alone in the guidance offices during the lunch hour. A 15-year-old girl in the tenth grade entered the office somewhat hesitantly. She told the intern that she had a problem and that she needed to talk to someone immediately. The counselor-in-training asked the girl to sit down and invited her to discuss her problem.

The student said that she would discuss her situation only if the counselor promised to keep the conversation completely confidential. The counselor agreed to do this.

The girl then proceeded to explain that she was in the fourth month of pregnancy. She had been "going steady" with a 17-year-old senior from a neighboring high school. Last night the girl's mother had confronted her with the fact that she was obviously pregnant.

She had acknowledged her pregnancy and her distraught mother called in the father. Her father went into a tirade of verbal abuse and, without listening to anything the girl had to say, announced that he would arrange for her to have an abortion. That morning the father told the daughter that he would take her that very evening to the office of a physician friend who had agreed to perform the abortion.

On the way to school the girl had called her boyfriend to tell him of the situation. They met during the morning, and the boyfriend told her that he would steal a car after school, meet her, and that they would run away together and try to be married in another state.

The girl presented her dilemma to the counselor and asked for help in deciding what to do.

The counselor was obviously confronted with a very complex ethical situation. She had made a promise of complete confidentiality. She now had knowledge of an impending abortion that was probably illegal and that was being forced on her client without any opportunity for counseling or even reflection. She also had knowledge of a probable car theft and a runaway situation involving two minors.

The counselor listened to the girl and asked her to return later, after lunch, for a regular appointment. In the interim she called her supervisor. Fortunately, it was possible for the supervisor to visit with the counselor-intern at the school immediately. In the ensuing supervisory session the intern went through the steps in the model described earlier.

In analyzing the situation the counselor decided that her behavior impacted on several people. Certainly her 15-year-old client would be affected. The client's mother and father, the boyfriend who was the prospective father, and the boy's parents were all also affected. In addition there was the question of the unborn child. Finally, the counselor felt a strong sense of responsibility to the school and to the profession that she was in the process of entering.

In reviewing the second-order principles that applied, the counselor identified the principle of *promise keeping*, the principle of *autonomy*, the principle of *parentalism*, and the *sanctity-of-life* principle as being relevant.

As the counselor discussed the situation with her supervisor, she decided that for her the sanctity-of-life principle was paramount. She believed that not only did the impending abortion constitute an illegal taking of the life of the fetus but that it also presented a probable threat to the girl's life because the operation would be done in a physician's office by a doctor apparently willing to perform an illegal abortion. Similarly, the counselor felt that the runaway option being considered might well end in a life-threatening situation for both teenagers if they wound up alone and destitute on the streets of a strange city.

The counselor also viewed as important the principle of autonomy in that her client had been given virtually no opportunity to think through her options and to make her own decisions. Both of the available options were being forced on her with little time or opportunity to decide.

Finally, the counselor, looking at the tender age of her client, felt that the girl needed protection and that since the natural parents were apparently not providing that protection, she, the counselor, was obligated to perform a "parental" or protective function.

As the counselor considered these principles and the values they implied, she weighed them against the principle of *promise keeping*.

Before we continue the case history, how would you the reader weigh the principles involved? What values would you seek to protect or enhance? Are there important considerations, principles, or people that the counselor has not thought about?

At this point the counselor decided that her primary goal was to prevent her client from being coerced into either an immediate abortion or running away from home. Consequently, she developed the following approach.

In her interview that afternoon with her client, the counselor stated that she was unable to keep the promise of complete confidentiality made earlier. The counselor explained this as clearly and carefully as possible. She pointed out the risks to the client presented in either going through with the immediate abortion or in running away from home.

Instead, she proposed to accompany the girl to her home and force a joint conference with the mother and father. The client agreed somewhat reluctantly to this plan on realizing that the counselor was prepared to contact the parents unilaterally if she refused.

The counselor accompanied the youngster to her home, and a very tense and stormy conference ensued.

The father began by denouncing the counselor for interfering in a private family matter and in a blustering tone threatened all sorts of dire reprisals. The counselor held her ground, and much of the father's bluster subsided when she firmly announced that she would hold him responsible for the girl's health and safety and was prepared to report any violations of law that might occur.

At this point the counselor proposed that the girl be referred to a local private psychiatric clinic for counseling and evaluation, with the understanding that the family would be involved in the treatment and that the possibility of a therapeutic abortion for psychiatric reasons would be considered.

The counselor arranged for the referral and was able to obtain an appointment for the family the following day. At this point she terminated contact.

How do you react to the counselor's approach from an ethical standpoint?

1. Was she ethically right in breaking the client's confidence?
2. Should she have promised that confidence in the first place?
3. Was the counselor's overall action justified ethically?
4. Was the fact that the prospective father was virtually ignored justified?
5. Was the plan sound from a clinical and professional standpoint?
6. What kind of stresses or risks to the counselor were involved?
7. Would you find those risks tolerable and acceptable?
8. What other ethical alternatives could the counselor have chosen?

In the following chapter you will be presented with a number of other cases that have confronted counselors. These are presented very briefly, and you are left to think through each situation for yourself and to formulate *your own* plan of action. As you discuss these cases in your class or with your fellow students, try to think through carefully the bases on which you decide and act. When you find that others make different choices, try to understand also the ways in which they think about the issues, principles, and decisions involved. Try to follow the four-step model described earlier.

REFERENCES

Rest, J. (1984). Research on moral development: Implications for training psychologists. *The Counseling Psychologist, 12*, 19–30.

Steininger, M., Newell, J. D., & Garcia, L. T. (1984). *Ethical issues in psychology.* Homewood, IL: Dorsey Press.

Chapter Eight
Practical Case Situations

We encourage readers to analyze these cases using the following seven questions (which were also listed in the previous chapter).

1. How does the counselor's behavior impact on relevant others? Who? How? When? To what extent?

2. What are the second-order principles that apply to this situation? Which do I view as paramount or overriding in this situation?

3. What are the specific positive values that I would intend to maximize in this situation? What are the negatives that I would most wish to avoid?

4. What are the specific alternative courses of action open to me as a counselor in this situation? What are the probable consequences of each? For the counselor? For the client? For others?

5. How do these consequences compare in terms of the overriding principle that I have declared and the values that flow from that principle?

6. How can I develop a plan of action to implement my principles and values?

7. How can I act on these principles? What prices might I have to pay? How will my actions reflect on the profession and on my future practice?

One important value of analyzing complex ethical dilemmas is that the process itself may promote the cognitive development of the counselor. In order to achieve this goal the process of analysis should be characterized by a willingness to consider the validity of other people's perspectives, a willingness to discuss openly and examine one's own thinking in a nondefensive manner. Readers also need to suspend their own needs to evaluate and criticize in order to engage in an honest and genuine discussion of the many facets and perspectives of complex ethical dilemmas. By all means, readers should understand that the process of case analysis should not be considered an adversarial activity. Readers will gain much more through participating in a cooperative search for understanding rather than a debate about right and wrong with winners and losers.

CASE 1

Dr. Smith has his clients complete a personality test and an interest test at home. The secretary reads the instructions to the clients, and they are told to mail the answers and booklets to the counselor's office. He has the test scored, and then he gives the scores, profiles, and narrative interpretations to the clients. The clients are told that the test results "speak for themselves." The counselor makes these test scores available to the clients' employers on request. His rationale for this practice is based on the fact that employers pay the counselor's fees. If clients don't want the results forwarded to their employers, clients must pay the counselor's fees.

CASE 2

Little Johnny Samuels is in the second grade in a rural school in upstate New York. His teacher referred him to a counselor to help determine the possible cause of Johnny's reading problems. The teacher said that Johnny couldn't read, was hyperactive, and presented some obvious sight and hearing problems that had not been treated.

The counselor administered an individual intelligence test, a children's projective device, and a reading test. The results were sent to the teacher with a copy to the parents because the test results and clinical observations revealed clear signs that the child was both emotionally disturbed and neurologically impaired.

Later, another counselor read the report and noted several glaring errors. Out of professional courtesy, he removed the report from the child's school file and reevaluated the child. He then told the parents that the earlier report was correct as far as it went, but he needed to do a more extensive evaluation. He was pleased that he was able to smooth the whole matter over without embarrassing a colleague.

CASE 3

A counselor has been hired to provide counseling services, including evaluations, for the State Department of Criminal Justice and Prison Management. The counselor runs workshops on stress management, provides individual counseling, and evaluates guards and other officials who are having job difficulties.

During an individual session with the counselor, a male guard reported that he routinely drank moderate amounts of liquor and took barbiturates in order to cope with job-related stress. While under the influence of alcohol, he had a homosexual liaison with a prisoner, and he now realizes that he is gay and wants the counselor's help to locate a gay support group. The counselor referred him to a gay counselor who maintained a private practice in a nearby city. He reported the abuse of alcohol and the use of the barbiturates to the guard's superior. However, he didn't mention referring the guard to a gay counselor even though the prison regulations do not allow active homosexuals to function as prison guards.

CASE 4

A counselor, Ms. Anne Baxter, M.S., has just completed a brief (1-day) workshop on Rational Emotive Therapy (RET). She had decided to read a couple of additional books on the topic, and then she plans to discuss the approach with a local counselor whom she has once heard described as a capable Rational Emotive therapist.

A very inhibited adolescent male (age 19 years), Martin Cohen, was referred to Ms. Baxter by his professor/advisor because he was doing poorly in his academic work. Martin has exceptionally high SAT scores and reports to the counselor that he has strong needs to achieve well and doesn't think he can cope with his increasingly deteriorating academic performance. The counselor decides that Martin would be a prime candidate for RET. She begins her next session by explaining how Martin's irrational beliefs were at the heart of his problems and that she had just found a very good treatment, called RET, that would make Martin do much better in his classes. Martin left in a huff, saying that he thought Ms. Baxter was incompetent. Ms. Baxter called Martin's faculty advisor and asked for his assistance in getting Martin back into treatment.

CASE 5

A 20-year-old male named James Jefferson had lost one kidney and was in the hospital for dialysis. The family was quite poor but very close, with strong religious convictions. James's health was steadily deteriorating. He was in much pain, and family members were beginning to experience signs of serious stress reactions. The father approached James's counselor, Dr. Lynn Goldstein, and asked her to write a recommendation to the hospital medical ethics committee recommending that treatment be discontinued. Mr. Jefferson said that James's time had come, and he didn't want the hospital to do anything to interfere with God's will. Mr. Jefferson had discussed this matter with his son James, and even though James cried a lot, he agreed that it was God's will and he wanted to go to his "heavenly rest."

Dr. Goldstein refused, saying it would be just like murdering poor James. She exclaimed, "Who knows whether we have really exhausted all possible resources for treatment!"

CASE 6

Mary Louise is a sophomore at State University and is majoring in psychology. She is worried about her recent weight gain (20 pounds in 1 month). She also has difficulty in concentrating on her studies. She is seeking help to choose a career.

In the course of counseling, the counselor learns that Mary Louise lives with her large Catholic family in a nearby rural city. Her father is a prominent banker, and her mother is a housewife who is very active in community social affairs. Mary Louise reports being very worried about the welfare of her younger sister. On questioning, she revealed that her father sexually abused her about 5 years ago. He had been drinking and told Mary Louise that he wanted to have sexual relations with her because of her mother's frigidity. Mary Louise is now worried that he may try to have sexual relations with her younger sister. She said that the family would be ruined and her father would lose his job if any of this information became known in her community. She just wants to forget the whole experience and hopes that her sister will not allow their father to use her as he used Mary Louise.

The counselor discussed the issue with his supervisor, Ms. Alicia Gordon, who insisted that the counselor have Mary Louise report the situation to her mother. If she didn't agree to do so, the counselor would have to report the matter to the mother.

CASE 7

Mr. James Cattell had just been hired as a guidance counselor at Edwina, Iowa, Senior High School. The former counselor left him a letter that described "a serious problem" in the school.

The letter began, "I am writing to acquaint you with a case which deserves urgent attention. That of Charles Bronson. As you are no doubt aware, it has not been my custom to commit to writing anything of a confidential nature. I certainly abide by the ethical dicta of our professional organizations! Thence, you will find few notes concerning any work with Charles. Of necessity, then, I decided to send you a memorandum regarding 'The Case of Charles Bronson' so that you can save this boy from his destructive tendencies.

"After reading my memorandum, please call Monica Edwards, who is an outstanding student leader, and she will give you additional information about the causes of Charles' difficulties. Briefly, Monica believes that Charles' problems stem from an unhealthy relationship with an older girl in the school who also happens to be from a different cultural background. Charles is white and the girl is Hispanic!

"I have already called his parents several times to discuss his problems and I have talked to him about them. But neither parents nor child will heed my warning. They believe that Monica is a trouble maker and threaten to take me to court because of my conversations with Monica." Mr. Cattell was very concerned about the letter from the former counselor but was unsure if it would be appropriate to report him to the local ethics committee.

CASE 8

A professor who is a specialist in Behavioral Therapy proposed doing research on the relative effectiveness of two treatments for test anxiety. One involves cognitive behavioral strategies, and the other emphasizes skills training. Clients who come to the practicum counseling laboratory and training clinic will be assigned to the two treatments using a table of random numbers. A number of clients will also be part of a "waiting list" control group. A graduate student in counseling psychology, Jane Addams, was doing her doctoral-level practicum in the clinic, and she became quite alarmed when she heard of the proposed research. She would not treat her clients as guinea pigs! She argued that the goals regarding treatment of real clients are in conflict with the goals regarding counseling process and/or outcomes research.

CASE 9

Mrs. Jones, a sprightly lady of 82 years, asked to see the counselor in her retirement community. Her children were upset by her handling of her finances and by her involvement with a much younger man (aged 75 years). For her own sake, before she had squandered all of her estate, they wanted her to sign papers that made them trustees and/or guardians of her estate. Her counselor, Mrs. Tessie Pope, noted that Mrs. Jones seemed confused and unsure of herself. Mrs. Jones also reported having difficulty sleeping at night.

Mrs. Jones pleaded for help. "It's not fair! The money was left to me by my husband. I can spend it any way I want!"

The counselor thought Mrs. Jones could benefit from a brief course in financial management, or at least she needed to talk with a financial consultant. So Mrs. Pope proceeded to make the arrangements for her husband, who worked in the bank, to visit with Mrs. Jones. . . .

CASE 10

A client was referred to a counselor by the personnel office of a local factory. The referral said that the client, Ms. Daisy Douan, was having serious problems with her supervisor. The client was a some-what naive young woman who worked as an engineer in the local factory. She reported that she was routinely subjected to sexual harassment from her male colleagues. She begged the counselor to help her get medical leave with pay so that she could get out of this terrible situation. She wanted the counselor to complete forms that would attest to the fact that she was emotionally impaired due to sexual harassment on her job. The counselor thought that the client's story was probably true but felt that he couldn't ethically comply with her wishes because she needed treatment for serious emotional problems that were not related to the sexual harassment.

CASE 11

A counselor, Jim Burke, Ph.D., received a brochure in the mail from a colleague who was requesting referrals for a group therapy program for clients suffering from agoraphobia, loneliness, and social anxiety. The colleague, Ms. Ellen Partine, M.S., described herself as a psychotherapist with over 15 years' experience in effectively treating these psychological disorders. The brochure went on to report statements from former clients who attested to Ms. Partine's superb clinical skills and how they had personally benefited from her group therapy program.

The brochure described the cost of treatment as far below that of similar treatment programs. Moreover, if clients weren't satisfied with the program, they were guaranteed their money back.

In her letter to Mr. Burke, Ms. Partine further indicated that any referrals would be greatly appreciated, that she would give Dr. Burke 2% of the fees paid by clients that he referred to her.

CASE 12

A student, Joe Jackson, in a Ph.D. program in counseling psychology, heard that a fellow student, Anne Miller, was having sexual relations with Dr. Alan Bruckner, the director of the program. They were seen together at several local clubs. Dr. Bruckner was also responsible for recommending students for various intern sites. The student was upset but couldn't prove anything decisively regarding the supposed affair. However, when Anne Miller, who was ninth in a class of ten, was recommended for a prestigious intern site, Joe became very angry and went to the department chair and demanded that he overrule Dr. Bruckner's recommendation because it was obvious that Anne Miller couldn't possibly deserve to be recommended for such a prestigious internship site.

Appendix A:
Ethical Principles
of Psychologists

Ethical Principles of Psychologists

PREAMBLE

Psychologists respect the dignity and worth of the individual and strive for the preservation and protection of fundamental human rights. They are committed to increasing knowledge of human behavior and of people's understanding of themselves and others and to the utilization of such knowledge for the promotion of human welfare. While pursuing these objectives, they make every effort to protect the welfare of those who seek their services and of the research participants that may be the object of study. They use their skills only for purposes consistent with these values and do not knowingly permit their misuse by others. While demanding for themselves freedom of inquiry and communication, psychologists accept the responsibility this freedom requires: competence, objectivity in the application of skills, and concern for the best interests of clients, colleagues, students, research participants, and society. In the pursuit of these ideals, psychologists subscribe to principles in the following areas: 1. Responsibility, 2. Competence, 3. Moral and Legal Standards, 4. Public Statements, 5. Confidentiality, 6. Welfare of the Consumer, 7. Professional Relationships, 8. Assessment Techniques, 9. Research With Human Participants, and 10. Care and Use of Animals.

Acceptance of membership in the American Psychological Association commits the member to adherence to these principles.

Psychologists cooperate with duly constituted committees of the American Psychological Association, in particular, the Committee on Scientific and Professional Ethics and Conduct, by responding to inquiries promptly and completely. Members also respond promptly and completely to inquiries from duly constituted state association ethics committees and professional standards review committees.

Principle 1
RESPONSIBILITY

In providing services, psychologists maintain the highest standards of their profession. They accept responsibility for the consequences of their acts and make every effort to ensure that their services are used appropriately.

a. As scientists, psychologists accept responsibility for the selection of their research topics and the methods used in investigation, analysis, and reporting. They plan their research in ways to minimize the possibility that their findings will be misleading. They provide thorough discussion of the limitations of their data, especially where their work touches on social policy or might be construed to the detriment of persons in specific age, sex,

ethnic, socioeconomic, or other social groups. In publishing reports of their work, they never suppress disconfirming data, and they acknowledge the existence of alternative hypotheses and explanations of their findings. Psychologists take credit only for work they have actually done.

b. Psychologists clarify in advance with all appropriate persons and agencies the expectations for sharing and utilizing research data. They avoid relationships that may limit their objectivity or create a conflict of interest. Interference with the milieu in which data are collected is kept to a minimum.

c. Psychologists have the responsibility to attempt to prevent distortion, misuse, or suppression of psychological findings by the institution or agency of which they are employees.

d. As members of governmental or other organizational bodies, psychologists remain accountable as individuals to the highest standards of their profession.

e. As teachers, psychologists recognize their primary obligation to help others acquire knowledge and skill. They maintain high standards of scholarship by presenting psychological information objectively, fully, and accurately.

f. As practitioners, psychologists know that they bear a heavy social responsibility because their recommendations and professional actions may alter the lives of others. They are alert to personal, social, organizational, financial, or political situations and pressures that might lead to misuse of their influence.

This version of the Ethical Principles of Psychologists (formerly entitled Ethical Standards of Psychologists) was adopted by the American Psychological Association's Council of Representatives on January 24, 1981. The revised Ethical Principles contain both substantive and grammatical changes in each of the nine ethical principles constituting the Ethical Standards of Psychologists previously adopted by the Council of Representatives in 1979, plus a new tenth principle entitled Care and Use of Animals. Inquiries concerning the Ethical Principles of Psychologists should be addressed to the Administrative Officer for Ethics, American Psychological Association, 1200 Seventeenth Street, N.W., Washington, D.C. 20036.

These revised Ethical Principles apply to psychologists, to students of psychology, and to others who do work of a psychological nature under the supervision of a psychologist. They are also intended for the guidance of nonmembers of the Association who are engaged in psychological research or practice.

Any complaints of unethical conduct filed after January 24, 1981, shall be governed by this 1981 revision. However, conduct (a) complained about after January 24, 1981, but which occurred prior to that date, and (b) not considered unethical under prior versions of the principles but considered unethical under the 1981 revision, shall not be deemed a violation of ethical principles. Any complaints pending as of January 24, 1981, shall be governed either by the 1979 or by the 1981 version of the Ethical Principles, at the sound discretion of the Committee on Scientific and Professional Ethics and Conduct.

Principle 2
COMPETENCE

The maintenance of high standards of competence is a responsibility shared by all psychologists in the interest of the public and the profession as a whole. Psychologists recognize the boundaries of their competence and the limitations of their techniques. They only provide services and only use techniques for which they are qualified by training and experience. In those areas in which recognized standards do not yet exist, psychologists take whatever precautions are necessary to protect the welfare of their clients. They maintain knowledge of current scientific and professional information related to the services they render.

a. Psychologists accurately represent their competence, education, training, and experience. They claim as evidence of educational qualifications only those degrees obtained from institutions acceptable under the Bylaws and Rules of Council of the American Psychological Association.

b. As teachers, psychologists perform their duties on the basis of careful preparation so that their instruction is accurate, current, and scholarly.

c. Psychologists recognize the need for continuing education and are open to new procedures and changes in expectations and values over time.

d. Psychologists recognize differences among people, such as those that may be associated with age, sex, socioeconomic, and ethnic backgrounds. When necessary, they obtain training, experience, or counsel to assure competent service or research relating to such persons.

e. Psychologists responsible for decisions involving individuals or policies based on test results have an understanding of psychological or educational measurement, validation problems, and test research.

f. Psychologists recognize that personal problems and conflicts may interfere with professional effectiveness. Accordingly, they refrain from undertaking any activity in which their personal problems are likely to lead to inadequate performance or harm to a client, colleague, student, or research participant. If engaged in such activity when they become aware of their personal problems, they seek competent professional assistance to determine whether they should suspend, terminate, or limit the scope of their professional and/or scientific activities.

Principle 3
MORAL AND LEGAL STANDARDS

Psychologists' moral and ethical standards of behavior are a personal matter to the same degree as they are for any other citizen, except as these may compromise the fulfillment of their professional responsibilities or reduce the public trust in psychology and psychologists. Regarding their own behavior, psychologists are sensi-

tive to prevailing community standards and to the possible impact that conformity to or deviation from these standards may have upon the quality of their performance as psychologists. Psychologists are also aware of the possible impact of their public behavior upon the ability of colleagues to perform their professional duties.

a. As teachers, psychologists are aware of the fact that their personal values may affect the selection and presentation of instructional materials. When dealing with topics that may give offense, they recognize and respect the diverse attitudes that students may have toward such materials.

b. As employees or employers, psychologists do not engage in or condone practices that are inhumane or that result in illegal or unjustifiable actions. Such practices include, but are not limited to, those based on considerations of race, handicap, age, gender, sexual preference, religion, or national origin in hiring, promotion, or training.

c. In their professional roles, psychologists avoid any action that will violate or diminish the legal and civil rights of clients or of others who may be affected by their actions.

d. As practitioners and researchers, psychologists act in accord with Association standards and guidelines related to practice and to the conduct of research with human beings and animals. In the ordinary course of events, psychologists adhere to relevant governmental laws and institutional regulations. When federal, state, provincial, organizational, or institutional laws, regulations, or practices are in conflict with Association standards and guidelines, psychologists make known their commitment to Association standards and guidelines and, wherever possible, work toward a resolution of the conflict. Both practitioners and researchers are concerned with the development of such legal and quasi-legal regulations as best serve the public interest, and they work toward changing existing regulations that are not beneficial to the public interest.

Principle 4
PUBLIC STATEMENTS

Public statements, announcements of services, advertising, and promotional activities of psychologists serve the purpose of helping the public make informed judgments and choices. Psychologists represent accurately and objectively their professional qualifications, affiliations, and functions, as well as those of the institutions or organizations with which they or the statements may be associated. In public statements providing psychological information or professional opinions or providing information about the availability of psychological products, publications, and services, psychologists base their statements on scientifically acceptable psycholog-

ical findings and techniques with full recognition of the limits and uncertainties of such evidence.

a. When announcing or advertising professional services, psychologists may list the following information to describe the provider and services provided: name, highest relevant academic degree earned from a regionally accredited institution, date, type, and level of certification or licensure, diplomate status, APA membership status, address, telephone number, office hours, a brief listing of the type of psychological services offered, an appropriate presentation of fee information, foreign languages spoken, and policy with regard to third-party payments. Additional relevant or important consumer information may be included if not prohibited by other sections of these Ethical Principles.

b. In announcing or advertising the availability of psychological products, publications, or services, psychologists do not present their affiliation with any organization in a manner that falsely implies sponsorship or certification by that organization. In particular and for example, psychologists do not state APA membership or fellow status in a way to suggest that such status implies specialized professional competence or qualifications. Public statements include, but are not limited to, communication by means of periodical, book, list, directory, television, radio, or motion picture. They do not contain (i) a false, fraudulent, misleading, deceptive, or unfair statement; (ii) a misinterpretation of fact or a statement likely to mislead or deceive because in context it makes only a partial disclosure of relevant facts; (iii) a testimonial from a patient regarding the quality of a psychologists' services or products; (iv) a statement intended or likely to create false or unjustified expectations of favorable results; (v) a statement implying unusual, unique, or one-of-a-kind abilities; (vi) a statement intended or likely to appeal to a client's fears, anxieties, or emotions concerning the possible results of failure to obtain the offered services; (vii) a statement concerning the comparative desirability of offered services; (viii) a statement of direct solicitation of individual clients.

c. Psychologists do not compensate or give anything of value to a representative of the press, radio, television, or other communication medium in anticipation of or in return for professional publicity in a news item. A paid advertisement must be identified as such, unless it is apparent from the context that it is a paid advertisement. If communicated to the public by use of radio or television, an advertisement is prerecorded and approved for broadcast by the psychologist, and a recording of the actual transmission is retained by the psychologist.

d. Announcements or advertisements of "personal growth groups," clinics, and agencies give a clear statement of purpose and a clear description of the experiences to be provided. The education, training, and experience of the staff members are appropriately specified.

e. Psychologists associated with the development or promotion of psychological devices, books, or other products offered for commercial sale make reasonable efforts

to ensure that announcements and advertisements are presented in a professional, scientifically acceptable, and factually informative manner.

f. Psychologists do not participate for personal gain in commercial announcements or advertisements recommending to the public the purchase or use of proprietary or single-source products or services when that participation is based solely upon their identification as psychologists.

g. Psychologists present the science of psychology and offer their services, products, and publications fairly and accurately, avoiding misrepresentation through sensationalism, exaggeration, or superficiality. Psychologists are guided by the primary obligation to aid the public in developing informed judgments, opinions, and choices.

h. As teachers, psychologists ensure that statements in catalogs and course outlines are accurate and not misleading, particularly in terms of subject matter to be covered, bases for evaluating progress, and the nature of course experiences. Announcements, brochures, or advertisements describing workshops, seminars, or other educational programs accurately describe the audience for which the program is intended as well as eligibility requirements, educational objectives, and nature of the materials to be covered. These announcements also accurately represent the education, training, and experience of the psychologists presenting the programs and any fees involved.

i. Public announcements or advertisements soliciting research participants in which clinical services or other professional services are offered as an inducement make clear the nature of the services as well as the costs and other obligations to be accepted by participants in the research.

j. A psychologist accepts the obligation to correct others who represent the psychologist's professional qualifications, or associations with products or services, in a manner incompatible with these guidelines.

k. Individual diagnostic and therapeutic services are provided only in the context of a professional psychological relationship. When personal advice is given by means of public lectures or demonstrations, newspaper or magazine articles, radio or television programs, mail, or similar media, the psychologist utilizes the most current relevant data and exercises the highest level of professional judgment.

l. Products that are described or presented by means of public lectures or demonstrations, newspaper or magazine articles, radio or television programs, or similar media meet the same recognized standards as exist for products used in the context of a professional relationship.

Principle 5
CONFIDENTIALITY

Psychologists have a primary obligation to respect the confidentiality of information obtained from persons

Ethical Principles of Psychologists

127

in the course of their work as psychologists. They reveal such information to others only with the consent of the person or the person's legal representative, except in those unusual circumstances in which not to do so would result in clear danger to the person or to others. Where appropriate, psychologists inform their clients of the legal limits of confidentiality.

a. Information obtained in clinical or consulting relationships, or evaluative data concerning children, students, employees, and others, is discussed only for professional purposes and only with persons clearly concerned with the case. Written and oral reports present only data germane to the purposes of the evaluation, and every effort is made to avoid undue invasion of privacy.

b. Psychologists who present personal information obtained during the course of professional work in writings, lectures, or other public forums either obtain adequate prior consent to do so or adequately disguise all identifying information.

c. Psychologists make provisions for maintaining confidentiality in the storage and disposal of records.

d. When working with minors or other persons who are unable to give voluntary, informed consent, psychologists take special care to protect these persons' best interests.

Principle 6
WELFARE OF THE CONSUMER

Psychologists respect the integrity and protect the welfare of the people and groups with whom they work. When conflicts of interest arise between clients and psychologists' employing institutions, psychologists clarify the nature and direction of their loyalties and responsibilities and keep all parties informed of their commitments. Psychologists fully inform consumers as to the purpose and nature of an evaluative, treatment, educational, or training procedure, and they freely acknowledge that clients, students, or participants in research have freedom of choice with regard to participation.

a. Psychologists are continually cognizant of their own needs and of their potentially influential position vis-à-vis persons such as clients, students, and subordinates. They avoid exploiting the trust and dependency of such persons. Psychologists make every effort to avoid dual relationships that could impair their professional judgment or increase the risk of exploitation. Examples of such dual relationships include, but are not limited to, research with and treatment of employees, students, supervisees, close friends, or relatives. Sexual intimacies with clients are unethical.

b. When a psychologist agrees to provide services to a client at the request of a third party, the psychologist assumes the responsibility of clarifying the nature of the relationships to all parties concerned.

c. Where the demands of an organization require psy-

chologists to violate these Ethical Principles, psychologists clarify the nature of the conflict between the demands and these principles. They inform all parties of psychologists' ethical responsibilities and take appropriate action.

d. Psychologists make advance financial arrangements that safeguard the best interests of and are clearly understood by their clients. They neither give nor receive any remuneration for referring clients for professional services. They contribute a portion of their services to work for which they receive little or no financial return.

e. Psychologists terminate a clinical or consulting relationship when it is reasonably clear that the consumer is not benefiting from it. They offer to help the consumer locate alternative sources of assistance.

Principle 7
PROFESSIONAL RELATIONSHIPS

Psychologists act with due regard for the needs, special competencies, and obligations of their colleagues in psychology and other professions. They respect the prerogatives and obligations of the institutions or organizations with which these other colleagues are associated.

a. Psychologists understand the areas of competence of related professions. They make full use of all the professional, technical, and administrative resources that serve the best interests of consumers. The absence of formal relationships with other professional workers does not relieve psychologists of the responsibility of securing for their clients the best possible professional service, nor does it relieve them of the obligation to exercise foresight, diligence, and tact in obtaining the complementary or alternative assistance needed by clients.

b. Psychologists know and take into account the traditions and practices of other professional groups with whom they work and cooperate fully with such groups. If a person is receiving similar services from another professional, psychologists do not offer their own services directly to such a person. If a psychologist is contacted by a person who is already receiving similar services from another professional, the psychologist carefully considers that professional relationship and proceeds with caution and sensitivity to the therapeutic issues as well as the client's welfare. The psychologist discusses these issues with the client so as to minimize the risk of confusion and conflict.

c. Psychologists who employ or supervise other professionals or professionals in training accept the obligation to facilitate the further professional development of these individuals. They provide appropriate working conditions, timely evaluations, constructive consultation, and experience opportunities.

d. Psychologists do not exploit their professional relationships with clients, supervisees, students, employees, or research participants sexually or otherwise. Psychologists do not condone or engage in sexual harassment. Sexual harassment is defined as deliberate or repeated comments, gestures, or physical contacts of a sexual nature that are unwanted by the recipient.

e. In conducting research in institutions or organizations, psychologists secure appropriate authorization to conduct such research. They are aware of their obligations to future research workers and ensure that host institutions receive adequate information about the research and proper acknowledgment of their contributions.

f. Publication credit is assigned to those who have contributed to a publication in proportion to their professional contributions. Major contributions of a professional character made by several persons to a common project are recognized by joint authorship, with the individual who made the principal contribution listed first. Minor contributions of a professional character and extensive clerical or similar nonprofessional assistance may be acknowledged in footnotes or in an introductory statement. Acknowledgment through specific citations is made for unpublished as well as published material that has directly influenced the research or writing. Psychologists who compile and edit material of others for publication publish the material in the name of the originating group, if appropriate, with their own name appearing as chairperson or editor. All contributors are to be acknowledged and named.

g. When psychologists know of an ethical violation by another psychologist, and it seems appropriate, they informally attempt to resolve the issue by bringing the behavior to the attention of the psychologist. If the misconduct is of a minor nature and/or appears to be due to lack of sensitivity, knowledge, or experience, such an informal solution is usually appropriate. Such informal corrective efforts are made with sensitivity to any rights to confidentiality involved. If the violation does not seem amenable to an informal solution, or is of a more serious nature, psychologists bring it to the attention of the appropriate local, state, and/or national committee on professional ethics and conduct.

Principle 8
ASSESSMENT TECHNIQUES

In the development, publication, and utilization of psychological assessment techniques, psychologists make every effort to promote the welfare and best interests of the client. They guard against the misuse of assessment results. They respect the client's right to know the results, the interpretations made, and the bases for their conclusions and recommendations. Psychologists make every effort to maintain the security of tests and other assessment techniques within limits of legal mandates. They strive to ensure the appropriate use of assessment techniques by others.

a. In using assessment techniques, psychologists re-

spect the right of clients to have full explanations of the nature and purpose of the techniques in language the clients can understand, unless an explicit exception to this right has been agreed upon in advance. When the explanations are to be provided by others, psychologists establish procedures for ensuring the adequacy of these explanations.

b. Psychologists responsible for the development and standardization of psychological tests and other assessment techniques utilize established scientific procedures and observe the relevant APA standards.

c. In reporting assessment results, psychologists indicate any reservations that exist regarding validity or reliability because of the circumstances of the assessment or the inappropriateness of the norms for the person tested. Psychologists strive to ensure that the results of assessments and their interpretations are not misused by others.

d. Psychologists recognize that assessment results may become obsolete. They make every effort to avoid and prevent the misuse of obsolete measures.

e. Psychologists offering scoring and interpretation services are able to produce appropriate evidence for the validity of the programs and procedures used in arriving at interpretations. The public offering of an automated interpretation service is considered a professional-to-professional consultation. Psychologists make every effort to avoid misuse of assessment reports.

f. Psychologists do not encourage or promote the use of psychological assessment techniques by inappropriately trained or otherwise unqualified persons through teaching, sponsorship, or supervision.

Principle 9
RESEARCH WITH HUMAN PARTICIPANTS

The decision to undertake research rests upon a considered judgment by the individual psychologist about how best to contribute to psychological science and human welfare. Having made the decision to conduct research, the psychologist considers alternative directions in which research energies and resources might be invested. On the basis of this consideration, the psychologist carries out the investigation with respect and concern for the dignity and welfare of the people who participate and with cognizance of federal and state regulations and professional standards governing the conduct of research with human participants.

a. In planning a study, the investigator has the responsibility to make a careful evaluation of its ethical acceptability. To the extent that the weighing of scientific and human values suggests a compromise of any principle, the investigator incurs a correspondingly serious obligation to seek ethical advice and to observe stringent safeguards to protect the rights of human participants.

b. Considering whether a participant in a planned

study will be a "subject at risk" or a "subject at minimal risk," according to recognized standards, is of primary ethical concern to the investigator.

c. The investigator always retains the responsibility for ensuring ethical practice in research. The investigator is also responsible for the ethical treatment of research participants by collaborators, assistants, students, and employees, all of whom, however, incur similar obligations.

d. Except in minimal-risk research, the investigator establishes a clear and fair agreement with research participants, prior to their participation, that clarifies the obligations and responsibilities of each. The investigator has the obligation to honor all promises and commitments included in that agreement. The investigator informs the participants of all aspects of the research that might reasonably be expected to influence willingness to participate and explains all other aspects of the research about which the participants inquire. Failure to make full disclosure prior to obtaining informed consent requires additional safeguards to protect the welfare and dignity of the research participants. Research with children or with participants who have impairments that would limit understanding and/or communication requires special safeguarding procedures.

e. Methodological requirements of a study may make the use of concealment or deception necessary. Before conducting such a study, the investigator has a special responsibility to (i) determine whether the use of such techniques is justified by the study's prospective scientific, educational, or applied value; (ii) determine whether alternative procedures are available that do not use concealment or deception; and (iii) ensure that the participants are provided with sufficient explanation as soon as possible.

f. The investigator respects the individual's freedom to decline to participate in or to withdraw from the research at any time. The obligation to protect this freedom requires careful thought and consideration when the investigator is in a position of authority or influence over the participant. Such positions of authority include, but are not limited to, situations in which research participation is required as part of employment or in which the participant is a student, client, or employee of the investigator.

g. The investigator protects the participant from physical and mental discomfort, harm, and danger that may arise from research procedures. If risks of such consequences exist, the investigator informs the participant of that fact. Research procedures likely to cause serious or lasting harm to a participant are not used unless the failure to use these procedures might expose the participant to risk of greater harm, or unless the research has great potential benefit and fully informed and voluntary consent is obtained from each participant. The participant should be informed of procedures for contacting the investigator within a reasonable time period following participation should stress, potential harm, or related questions or concerns arise.

h. After the data are collected, the investigator provides the participant with information about the nature of the study and attempts to remove any misconceptions that may have arisen. Where scientific or humane values justify delaying or withholding this information, the investigator incurs a special responsibility to monitor the research and to ensure that there are no damaging consequences for the participant.

i. Where research procedures result in undesirable consequences for the individual participant, the investigator has the responsibility to detect and remove or correct these consequences, including long-term effects.

j. Information obtained about a research participant during the course of an investigation is confidential unless otherwise agreed upon in advance. When the possibility exists that others may obtain access to such information, this possibility, together with the plans for protecting confidentiality, is explained to the participant as part of the procedure for obtaining informed consent.

Principle 10
CARE AND USE OF ANIMALS

An investigator of animal behavior strives to advance understanding of basic behavioral principles and/or to contribute to the improvement of human health and welfare. In seeking these ends, the investigator ensures the welfare of animals and treats them humanely. Laws and regulations notwithstanding, an animal's immediate protection depends upon the scientist's own conscience.

a. The acquisition, care, use, and disposal of all animals are in compliance with current federal, state or provincial, and local laws and regulations.

b. A psychologist trained in research methods and experienced in the care of laboratory animals closely supervises all procedures involving animals and is responsible for ensuring appropriate consideration of their comfort, health, and humane treatment.

c. Psychologists ensure that all individuals using animals under their supervision have received explicit instruction in experimental methods and in the care, maintenance, and handling of the species being used. Responsibilities and activities of individuals participating in a research project are consistent with their respective competencies.

d. Psychologists make every effort to minimize discomfort, illness, and pain of animals. A procedure subjecting animals to pain, stress, or privation is used only when an alternative procedure is unavailable and the goal is justified by its prospective scientific, educational, or applied value. Surgical procedures are performed under appropriate anesthesia; techniques to avoid infection and minimize pain are followed during and after surgery.

e. When it is appropriate that the animal's life be terminated, it is done rapidly and painlessly.

Appendix B: Standards for Providers of Psychological Services

In January 1975, the APA Council of Representatives created the original Committee on Standards for Providers of Psychological Services. The Committee was charged with updating and revising the Standards adopted in September 1974. Members of the Committee were Jacqueline C. Bouhoutsos, Leon Hall, Marian D. Hall, Mary Henle, Durand F. Jacobs (Chair), Abel Ossorio, and Wayne Sorenson. Task force liaison was Jerry H. Clark, and Central Office liaison was Arthur Centor.

In January 1976, Council further charged the Committee to review the Standards and recommend revisions needed to reflect the varying needs of only those psychologists engaged in the activities of clinical, counseling, industrial-organizational, and school psychology. The Committee was reconstituted with one member representing each of the four applied activities, plus one member representing institutional practice and one representing the public interest.

Members were Jules Barron, clinical; Barbara A. Kirk, counseling; Frank Friedlander, industrial-organizational (replacing Virginia Schein); Durand F. Jacobs (Chair), institutional practice; M. Brewster Smith, public interest; Marian D. Hall, school; Arthur Centor was Central Office liaison.

Published by
American Psychological Association, Inc.
1200 Seventeenth Street, N.W.
Washington, D.C. 20036 Copyright ©1977
by the American Psychological Association.
All rights reserved.

Standards for Providers of

Psychological Services

The Standards that follow are the first revision of the national Standards for Providers of Psychological Services originally adopted by the American Psychological Association (APA) on September 4, 1974.[1] **[Note: Footnotes 2–24 appear at the end of the Standards. See pp. 11–14.]** The intent of these Standards is to improve the quality, effectiveness, and accessibility of psychological services to all who require them.[2]

These Standards represent the attainment of a goal for which the Association has striven for over 20 years, namely, to codify a uniform set of standards for psychological practice that would serve the respective needs of users, providers, and third-party purchasers and sanctioners of psychological services. In addition, the Association has established a standing committee charged with keeping the Standards responsive to the needs of these groups and with upgrading and extending them progressively as the profession and science of psychology con-

tinue to develop new knowledge, improved methods, and additional modes of psychological service. These Standards have been established by organized psychology as a means of self-regulation to protect the public interest.

While these revised Standards contain a number of important changes, they differ from the original Standards in two major respects:

1. They uniformly specify the *minimally acceptable levels* of quality assurance and performance that providers of those psychological services covered by the Standards must reach or exceed. Care has been taken to assure that each standard is clearly stated, readily measurable, realistic, and implementable.

2. The revised Standards apply to a more limited range of services than the original Standards. The present Standards have been restricted to applications in "human services" with the goal of facilitating more effective human functioning. The kinds of psychological services covered by the present Standards are those ordinarily involved in the practice of specialists in clinical, counseling, industrial-organizational, and school psychology. However, it is important to note that these Standards cover psychological *functions* and not classes of practitioners.

Any persons representing themselves as psychologists, when providing any of the covered psychological service functions at

---

[1] Members of the Task Force on Standards for Service Facilities that submitted the original Standards in September 1974 were Milton L. Blum, Jacqueline C. Bouhoutsos, Jerry H. Clark, Harold A. Edgerton, Marian D. Hall, Durand F. Jacobs (Chair, 1972–1974), Floyd H. Martinez, John E. Muthard, Asher R. Pacht, William D. Pierce, Sue A. Warren, and Alfred M. Wellner (Chair, 1970–1971). Staff liaisons from the APA Office of Professional Affairs were John J. McMillan (1970–1971), Gottlieb C. Simon (1971–1973), and Arthur Centor (1973–1974).

2   STANDARDS FOR PROVIDERS

any time and in any setting, whether public or private, profit or nonprofit, are required to observe these standards of practice in order to promote the best interests and welfare of the users of such services. It is to be understood that fulfillment of the requirements to meet these Standards shall be judged by peers in relation to the capabilities for evaluation and the circumstances that prevail in the setting at the time the program or service is evaluated.

Standards covering other psychological service functions may be added from time to time to those already listed. However, functions and activities related to the teaching of psychology, the writing or editing of scholarly or scientific manuscripts, and the conduct of scientific research do not fall within the purview of the present Standards.

Historical Background

Early in 1970, acting at the direction of the Association's Council of Representatives, the Board of Professional Affairs appointed a Task Force composed of practicing psychologists with specialized knowledge in at least one of every major class of human service facility and with experience relevant to the setting of standards. Its charge was to develop a set of standards for psychological practice. Soon thereafter, partial support for this activity was obtained through a grant from the National Institute of Mental Health.[3]

First, the Task Force established liaison with national groups already active in standard setting and accreditation. It was therefore able to influence the adoption of certain basic principles and wording contained in standards for psychological services published by the Joint Commission on Accreditation of Hospitals (JCAH) Accreditation Council for Facilities for the Mentally Retarded (1971) and by the Accreditation Council for Psychiatric Facilities (JCAH, 1972). It also contributed substantially to the "constitutionally required minimum standards for adequate treatment of

the mentally ill" ordered by the U.S. District Court in Alabama (*Wyatt v. Stickney*, 1972). In concert with other APA committees, the Task Force also represented the Association in national-level deliberations with governmental groups and insurance carriers that defined the qualifications necessary for psychologists involved in providing health services.

These interim outcomes involved influence by the Association on actions by groups of nonpsychologists that directly affected the manner in which psychological services were employed, particularly in health and rehabilitation settings. However, these measures did not relieve the Association from exercising its responsibility to speak out directly and authoritatively on what standards for psychological practice should be throughout a broad range of human service settings. It was also the responsibility of the Association to determine how psychologists would be held accountable should their practice fail to meet quality standards.

In September 1974, after more than 4 years of study and broad consultations, the Task Force proposed a set of standards, which the Association's Council of Representatives adopted and voted to publish in order to meet urgent needs of the public and the profession. Members of Council had various reservations about the scope and wording of the Standards as initially adopted. By establishing a continuing Committee on Standards, Council took the first step in what would be an ongoing process of review and revision.

The task of collecting, analyzing, and synthesizing reactions to the original Standards fell to two successive committees. They were charged similarly to review and revise the Standards and to suggest means to implement them, including their acceptance by relevant governmental and private accreditation groups. The dedicated work of the psychologists who served on both those committees is gratefully acknowledged. Also recognized with thanks are the several hundred comments received from scores of interested persons representing professional, academic, and scientific psychology, consumer groups, administrators of facilities, and others. This input from those directly affected by the original Standards provided the major stimulus and much of the content for the changes that appear in this revision.

Principles and Implications of Standards

A few basic principles have guided the development of these Standards:

1. There should be a single set of standards that governs psychological service functions offered by psychologists, regardless of their specialty, setting, or form of remuneration. All psychologists in professional practice should be guided by a uniform set of standards just as they are guided by a common code of ethics.

2. Standards should clearly establish minimally acceptable levels of quality for covered psychological service functions, regardless of the character of the users, purchasers, or sanctioners of such covered services.

3. All persons providing psychological services shall meet minimally acceptable levels of training and experience, which are consistent and appropriate with the functions they perform. However, final responsibility and accountability for services provided must rest with psychologists who have earned a doctoral degree in a program that is primarily psychological at a regionally accredited university or professional school. Those providing psychological services who have lesser (or other) levels of training shall be supervised by a psychologist with the above training. This level of qualification is necessary to assure that the public receives services of high quality.

4. There should be a uniform set of standards governing the quality of services to all users of psychological services in both the private and public sectors. There is no justification for maintaining the double standard presently embedded in most state legislation whereby providers of private fee-based psychological services are subject to statutory regulation, while those providing similar psychological services under governmental auspices are usually exempt from such regulations. This circumstance tends to afford greater protection

under the law for those receiving privately delivered psychological services. On the other hand, those receiving privately delivered psychological services currently lack many of the safeguards that are available in governmental settings; these include peer review, consultation, record review, and staff supervision.

5. While assuring the user of the psychologist's accountability for the nature and quality of services rendered, standards must not constrain the psychologist from employing new methods or making flexible use of support personnel in staffing the delivery of services.

The Standards here presented have broad implications both for the public who use psychological services and for providers of such services:

1. Standards provide a firmer basis for a mutual understanding between provider and user and facilitate more effective evaluation of services provided and outcomes achieved.

2. Standards are an important step toward greater uniformity in legislative and regulatory actions involving providers of psychological services, and Standards provide the basis for the development of accreditation procedures for service facilities.

3. Standards give specific content to the profession's concept of ethical practice.

4. Standards have significant impact on tomorrow's training models for both professional and support personnel in psychology.

5. Standards for the provision of psychological services in human service facilities influence what is considered acceptable structure, budgeting, and staffing patterns in these facilities.

6. Standards are living documents that require continual review and revision.

The Standards illuminate weaknesses in the delivery of psychological services and point to their correction. Some settings are known to require additional and/or higher standards for specific areas of service delivery than those herein proposed. There is no intent to diminish

4   STANDARDS FOR PROVIDERS

the scope or quality of psychological services that exceed these Standards.

Systematically applied, these Standards serve to establish uniformly the *minimally acceptable levels* of psychological services. They serve to establish a more effective and consistent basis for evaluating the performance of individual service providers, and they serve to guide the organizing of psychological service units in human service settings.

Definitions

Providers of psychological services refers to the following persons:

A. Professional psychologists.[4] Professional psychologists have a doctoral degree from a regionally accredited university or professional school in a program that is primarily psychological[5] and appropriate training and experience in the area of service offered.[6]

B. All other persons who offer psychological services under the supervision of a professional psychologist.

Psychological services refers to one or more of the following:[7]

A. Evaluation, diagnosis, and assessment of the functioning of individuals and groups in a variety of settings and activities.

B. Interventions to facilitate the functioning of individuals and groups. Such interventions may include psychological counseling, psychotherapy, and process consultation.

C. Consultation relating to A and B above.

D. Program development services in the areas of A, B, and C above.[8]

E. Supervision of psychological services.

A *psychological service unit* is the functional unit through which psychological services are provided:

A. A psychological service unit is a unit that provides predominantly psychological services and is composed of one or more professional psychologists and supporting staff.

B. A psychological service unit may operate as a professional service or as a functional or

geographic component of a larger governmental, educational, correction, health, training, industrial, or commercial organizational unit.[9]

C. A psychologist providing professional services in a multioccupational setting is regarded as a psychological service unit.

D. A psychological service unit also may be an individual or group of individuals in a private practice or a psychological consulting firm.

User includes:

A. Direct users or recipients of psychological services.

B. Public and private institutions, facilities, or organizations receiving psychological services.

C. Third-party purchasers—those who pay for the delivery of services but who are not the recipients of services.

Sanctioners refers to those users and nonusers who have a legitimate concern with the accessibility, timeliness, efficacy, and standards of quality attending the provision of psychological services. In addition to the users, sanctioners may include members of the user's family, the court, the probation officer, the school administrator, the employer, the union representative, the facility director, etc. Another class of sanctioners is represented by various governmental, peer review, and accreditation bodies concerned with the assurance of quality.

Standard 1. Providers

1.1 *Each psychological service unit offering psychological services shall have available at least one professional psychologist and as many more professional psychologists as are necessary to assure the quality of services offered.*

INTERPRETATION: The intent of this Standard is that one or more providers of psychological services in any psychological service unit shall meet the levels of training and experience of the professional psychologist as specified in the preceding definitions.[10]

When a professional psychologist is not available on a full-time basis, the facility shall retain the services of one or more professional psychologists on a regular part-time basis to supervise the psychological services provided. The psychologist(s) so retained shall have authority and participate sufficiently to enable him or her to assess the needs for services, review the content of services provided, and assume professional responsibility and accountability for them.

1.2 *Providers of psychological services who do not meet the requirements for the professional psychologist shall be supervised by a professional psychologist who shall assume professional responsibility and accountability for the services provided. The level and extent of supervision may vary from task to task so long as the supervising psychologist retains a sufficiently close supervisory relationship to meet this standard.*

1.3 *Wherever a psychological service unit exists, a professional psychologist shall be responsible for planning, directing, and reviewing the provision of psychological services.*

INTERPRETATION: This psychologist shall coordinate the activities of the psychological service unit with other professional, administrative, and technical groups, both within and outside the facility. This psychologist, who may be the director, chief, or coordinator of the psychological service unit, has related responsibilities including, but not limited to, recruiting qualified staff, directing training and research activities of the service, maintaining a high level of professional and ethical practice, and assuring that staff members function only within the areas of their competency.

In order to facilitate the effectiveness of services by increasing the level of staff sensitivity and professional skills, the psychologist designated as director shall be responsible for participating in the selection of the staff and sup-

porting personnel whose qualifications and skills (e.g., language, cultural and experiential background, race, and sex) are directly relevant to the needs and characteristics of the users served.

1.4 *When functioning as part of an organizational setting, professional psychologists shall bring their background and skills to bear whenever appropriate upon the goals of the organization by participating in the planning and development of overall services.*[11]

INTERPRETATION: Professional psychologists shall participate in the maintenance of high professional standards by representation on committees concerned with service delivery.

As appropriate to the setting, these activities may include active participation, as voting and as office-holding members on the facility's executive, planning, and evaluation boards and committees.

1.5 *Psychologists shall maintain current knowledge of scientific and professional developments that are directly related to the services they render.*

INTERPRETATION: Methods through which knowledge of scientific and professional development may be gained include, but are not limited to, continuing education, attendance at workshops, participation in staff development, and reading scientific publications.[12]

The psychologist shall have ready access to reference material related to the provision of psychological services.

Psychologists must be prepared to show evidence periodically that they are staying abreast of current knowledge and practices through continuing education.

1.6 *Psychologists shall limit their practice to their demonstrated areas of professional competence.*

INTERPRETATION: Psychological services will be offered in accordance with the provider's areas of competence as defined by verifiable training and experience. When extending services beyond the range of their usual practice, psychologists shall obtain pertinent training or appropriate professional supervision.

1.7 *Psychologists who wish to change their service specialty or to add an additional area of applied specialization must meet the same requirements with respect to subject matter and professional skills that apply to doctoral training in the new specialty.* [13]

INTERPRETATION: Training of doctoral-level psychologists to qualify them for change in specialty will be under the auspices of accredited university departments or professional schools that offer the doctoral degree in that specialty. Such training should be individualized, due credit being given for relevant coursework or requirements that have previously been satisfied. Merely taking an internship or acquiring experience in a practicum setting is not considered adequate preparation for becoming a clinical, counseling, industrial-organizational, or school psychologist when prior training has not been in the relevant area. Fulfillment of such an individualized training program is attested to by the award of a certificate by the supervising department or professional school indicating the successful completion of preparation in the particular specialty.

Standard 2. Programs

2.1 *Composition and organization of a psychological service unit:*

　　2.1.1 *The composition and programs of a psychological service unit shall be responsive to the needs of the persons or settings served.*

INTERPRETATION: A psychological service unit shall be so structured as to facilitate effective and economical delivery of services. For example, a psychological service unit serving a predominantly low-income, ethnic, or racial minority group should have a staffing pattern and service program that is adapted to the linguistic, experiential, and attitudinal characteristics of the users.

　　2.1.2 *A description of the organization of the psychological service unit and its lines of responsibility and accountability for the delivery of psychological services shall be available in written form to staff of the unit and to users and sanctioners upon request.*

INTERPRETATION: The description should include lines of responsibility, supervisory relationships, and the level and extent of accountability for each person who provides psychological services.

　　2.1.3 *A psychological service unit shall include sufficient numbers of professional and support personnel to achieve its goals, objectives, and purposes.*

INTERPRETATION: The workload and diversity of psychological services required and the specific goals and objectives of the setting will determine the numbers and qualifications of professional and support personnel in the psychological service unit. Where shortages in personnel exist so that psychological services cannot be rendered in a professional manner, the director of the psychological service unit shall initiate action to modify appropriately the specific goals and objectives of the service.

2.2 *Policies:*

　　2.2.1 *When the psychological service unit is composed of more than one person wherein a supervisory relationship exists or is a component of a larger organization, a written statement of its objectives and scope of services shall be developed and maintained.*

INTERPRETATION: The psychological service unit shall review its objectives and scope of services annually and revise them as necessary to insure that the psychological services offered are consistent with staff competencies and current psychological knowledge and practice. This statement should be distributed to staff and, where appropriate, to users and sanctioners upon request.

icy statements relevant to standards for professional services issued by the Association.

INTERPRETATION: Providers of psychological services, users, and sanctioners may order copies of these documents from the American Psychological Association.

2.2.2. *All providers within a psychological service unit shall support the legal and civil rights of the user.*[14]

INTERPRETATION: Providers of psychological services shall safeguard the interests of the user with regard to personal, legal, and civil rights. They shall continually be sensitive to the issue of confidentiality of information, the short-term and long-term impact of their decisions and recommendations, and other matters pertaining to individual, legal, and civil rights. Concerns regarding the safeguarding of individual rights of users include, but are not limited to, problems of self-incrimination in judicial proceedings, involuntary commitment to hospitals, protection of minors or legal incompetents, discriminatory practices in employment selection procedures, recommendations for special education provisions, information relative to adverse personnel actions in the armed services, and the adjudication of domestic relations disputes in divorce and custodial proceedings. Providers of psychological services should take affirmative action by making themselves available for local committees, review boards, and similar advisory groups established to safeguard the human, civil, and legal rights of service users.

2.2.3 *All providers within a psychological service unit shall be familiar with and adhere to the American Psychological Association's* Ethical Standards of Psychologists, Psychology as a Profession, Standards for Educational and Psychological Tests, *and other official pol-*

2.2.4 *All providers within a psychological service unit shall conform to relevant statutes established by federal, state, and local governments.*

INTERPRETATION: All providers of psychological services shall be familiar with appropriate statutes regulating the practice of psyehology. They shall also be informed about agency regulations that have the force of law and that relate to the delivery of psychological services (e.g., evaluation for disability retirement and special education placements). In addition, all providers shall be cognizant that federal agencies such as the Veterans Administration and the Department of Health, Education, and Welfare have policy statements regarding psychological services. Providers of psychological services shall be familiar with other statutes and regulations, including those addressed to the civil and legal rights of users (e.g., those promulgated by the federal Equal Employment Opportunity Commission) that are pertinent to their scope of practice.

It shall be the responsibility of the American Psychological Association to publish periodically those federal policies, statutes, and regulations relating to this section. The state psychological associations are similarly urged to publish and distribute periodically appropriate state statutes and regulations.

2.2.5 *All providers within a psychological service unit shall, where appropriate, inform themselves about and use the network of human services in their com-*

munities in order to link users with relevant services and resources.

INTERPRETATION: It is incumbent upon psychologists and supporting staff to be sensitive to the broader context of human needs. In recognizing the matrix of personal and societal problems, providers shall, where appropriate, make available information regarding human services such as legal aid societies, social services, employment agencies, health resources, and educational and recreational facilities. The provider of psychological services shall refer to such community resources and, when indicated, actively intervene on behalf of the user.

2.2.6 *In the delivery of psychological services, the providers shall maintain a continuing cooperative relationship with colleagues and co-workers whenever in the best interest of the user.*[15]

INTERPRETATION: It shall be the responsibility of the psychologist to recognize the areas of special competence of other psychologists and of other professionals for either consultation or referral purposes. Providers of psychological services shall make appropriate use of other professional, technical, and administrative resources whenever these serve the best interests of the user, and shall establish and maintain cooperative arrangements with such other resources as required to meet the needs of users.

2.3 *Procedures:*

2.3.1 *Where appropriate, each psychological service unit shall be guided by a set of procedural guidelines for the delivery of psychological services. If appropriate to the setting, these guidelines shall be in written form.*

INTERPRETATION: Depending on the nature of the setting, and whenever feasible, providers

should be prepared to provide a statement of procedural guidelines in either oral or written form that can be understood by users as well as sanctioners. This statement may describe the current methods, forms, procedures, and techniques being used to achieve the objectives and goals for psychological services.

This statement shall be communicated to staff and, when appropriate, to users and sanctioners. The psychological service unit shall provide for the annual review of its procedures for the delivery of psychological services.

2.3.2. *Providers shall develop a plan appropriate to the provider's professional strategy of practice and to the problems presented by the user.*

INTERPRETATION: Whenever appropriate or mandated in the setting, this plan shall be in written form as a means of providing a basis for establishing accountability, obtaining informed consent, and providing a mechanism for subsequent peer review. Regardless of the type of setting or users involved, it is desirable that a plan be developed that describes the psychological services indicated and the manner in which they will be provided.[16]

A psychologist who provides services as one member of a collaborative effort shall participate in the development and implementation of the overall service plan and provide for its periodic review.

2.3.3 *There shall be a mutually acceptable understanding between the provider and user or responsible agent regarding the delivery of service.*

INTERPRETATION: Varying service settings call for understandings differing in explicitness and formality. For instance, a psychologist providing services within a user organization may operate within a broad framework of understanding with this organization as a condition of employment. As another example, psychologists providing professional services to individuals in clinical, counseling, or school settings require an open-ended agreement, which specifies procedures and their known risks (if any), costs, and respective responsibilities of provider and user for achieving the agreed-upon objectives.

> 2.3.4   *Accurate, current, and pertinent documentation shall be made of essential psychological services provided.*

INTERPRETATION: Records kept of psychological services may include, but not be limited to, identifying data, dates of services, types of services, and significant actions taken. Providers of psychological services shall insure that essential information concerning services rendered is appropriately recorded within a reasonable time of their completion.

> 2.3.5   *Providers of psychological services shall establish a system to protect confidentiality of their records.*[17]

INTERPRETATION: Psychologists are responsible for maintaining the confidentiality of information about users of services whether obtained by themselves or by those they supervise. All persons supervised by psychologists, including nonprofessional personnel and students, who have access to records of psychological services shall be required to maintain this confidentiality as a condition of employment.

The psychologist shall not release confidential information, except with the written consent of the user directly involved or his or her legal representative. Even after the consent has been obtained for release, the psychologist should clearly identify such information as confidential to the recipient of the information.[18] If directed otherwise by statute or regulations with the force of law or by court order, the psychologist shall seek a resolution to the conflict that is both ethically and legally feasible and appropriate.

Users shall be informed in advance of any limits in the setting for maintenance of confidentiality of psychological information. For instance, psychologists in hospital settings shall inform their patients that psychological information in a patient's clinical record may be available without the patient's written consent to other members of the professional staff associated with the patient's treatment or rehabilitation. Similar limitations on confidentiality of psychological information may be present in certain school, industrial, or military settings, or in instances where the user has waived confidentiality for purposes of third-party payment.

When the user intends to waive confidentiality, the psychologist should discuss the implications of releasing psychological information, and assist the user in limiting disclosure only to information required by the present circumstance.

Raw psychological data (e.g., test protocols, therapy or interview notes, or questionnaire returns) in which a user is identified shall be released only with the written consent of the user or legal representative and released only to a person recognized by the psychologist as competent to use the data.

Any use made of psychological reports, records, or data for research or training purposes shall be consistent with this Standard. Additionally, providers of psychological services shall comply with statutory confidentiality requirements and those embodied in the American Psychological Association's *Ethical Standards of Psychologists* (APA, 1977).

Providers of psychological services should remain sensitive to both the benefits and the possible misuse of information regarding individuals that is stored in large computerized data banks. Providers should use their influence to ensure that such information is used in a socially responsible manner.

Standard 3. Accountability

> 3.1   *Psychologists' professional activity shall be primarily guided by the principle of promoting human welfare.*

INTERPRETATION: Psychologists shall provide services to users in a manner that is considerate, effective, and economical.

Psychologists are responsible for making their services readily accessible to users in a manner that facilitates the user's freedom of choice.

Psychologists shall be mindful of their accountability to the sanctioners of psychological services and to the general public, provided that appropriate steps are taken to protect the confidentiality of the service relationship. In the pursuit of their professional activities they shall aid in the conservation of human, material, and financial resources.

The psychological service unit will not withhold services to a potential client on the basis of that user's race, color, religion, sex, age, or national origin. Recognition is given, however, to the following considerations: The professional right of psychologists to limit their practice to a specific category of user (e.g., children, adolescents, women); the right and responsibility of psychologists to withhold an assessment procedure when not validly applicable; the right and responsibility of psychologists to withhold evaluative, psychotherapeutic, counseling, or other services in specific instances where considerations of race, religion, color, sex, or any other difference between psychologist and client might impair the effectiveness of the relationship.[19]

Psychologists who find that psychological services are being provided in a manner that is discriminatory or exploitative to users and/or contrary to these Standards or to state or federal statutes shall take appropriate corrective action, which may include the refusal to provide services. When conflicts of interest arise, the psychologist shall be guided in the resolution of differences by the principles set forth in the *Ethical Standards of Psychologists* of the American Psychological Association and by the Guidelines for Conditions of Employment of Psychologists (1972).[20]

3.2   *Psychologists shall pursue their activities as members of an independent, autonomous profession.*[21]

INTERPRETATION: Psychologists shall be aware of the implications of their activities for the profession as a whole. They shall seek to eliminate discriminatory practices instituted for self-serving purposes that are not in the interest of the user (e.g., arbitrary requirements for referral and supervision by another profession). They shall be cognizant of their responsibilities for the development of the profession, participate where possible in the training and career development of students and other providers, participate as appropriate in the training of paraprofessionals, and integrate and supervise their contributions within the structure established for delivering psychological services. Where appropriate, they shall facilitate the development of, and participate in, professional standards review mechanisms.[22]

Psychologists shall seek to work with other professionals in a cooperative manner for the good of the user and the benefit of the general public. Psychologists associated with multidisciplinary settings shall support the principle that members of each participating profession shall have equal rights and opportunities to share all privileges and responsibilities of full membership in the human service facility, and to administer service programs in their respective areas of competence.

3.3   *There shall be periodic, systematic, and effective evaluations of psychological services.*[23]

INTERPRETATION: When the psychological service unit is a component of a larger organization, regular assessment of progress in achieving goals shall be provided in the service delivery plan, including consideration of the effectiveness of psychological services relative to costs in terms of time, money, and the availability of professional and support personnel.

Evaluation of the efficiency and effectiveness of the psychological service delivery system should be conducted internally and, when possible, under independent auspices.

It is highly desirable that there be a periodic reexamination of review mechanisms to ensure that these attempts at public safeguards are effective and cost efficient and do not place unnecessary encumbrances on the provider or unnecessary additional expense to users or sanctioners for services rendered.

3.4 *Psychologists are accountable for all aspects of the services they provide and
shall be responsive to those concerned
with these services.* [24]

INTERPRETATION: In recognizing their responsibilities to users, sanctioners, third-party
purchasers, and other providers, wherever appropriate and consistent with the user's legal
rights and privileged communications, psychologists shall make available information
about, and opportunity to participate in, decisions concerning such issues as initiation, termination, continuation, modification, and
evaluation of psychological services. Additional copies of these *Standards for Providers
of Psychological Services* can be ordered from
the American Psychological Association.

Depending upon the settings, accurate and
full information shall be made available to prospective individual or organization users regarding the qualifications of providers, the nature and extent of services offered, and, where
appropriate, financial and social costs.

Where appropriate, psychologists shall inform users of their payment policies and their
willingness to assist in obtaining reimbursement. Those who accept reimbursement from a
third party should be acquainted with the appropriate statutes and regulations and should
instruct their users on proper procedures for
submitting claims and limits on confidentiality
of claims information, in accordance with pertinent statutes.

Standard 4. Environment

4.1 *Providers of psychological services shall
promote the development in the service
setting of a physical, organizational, and
social environment that facilitates optimal human functioning.*

INTERPRETATION: Federal, state, and local
requirements for safety, health, and sanitation
must be observed. Attention shall be given to
the comfort and, where relevant, to the privacy
of providers and users.

As providers of services, psychologists have
the responsibility to be concerned with the environment of their service unit, especially as it
affects the quality of service, but also as it impinges on human functioning in the larger unit
or organization when the service unit is included in such a larger context. Physical arrangements and organizational policies and
procedures should be conducive to the human
dignity, self-respect, and optimal functioning
of users, and to the effective delivery of service. The atmosphere in which psychological
services are rendered should be appropriate to
the service and to the users, whether in office,
clinic, school, or industrial organization.

NOTES

[2] The footnotes appended to these Standards represent an attempt to provide a coherent context of
other policy statements of the Association regarding
professional practice. The Standards extend these
previous policy statements where necessary to reflect
current concerns of the public and the profession.

[3] NIMH Grant MH 21696.

[4] For the purpose of transition, persons who met
the following criteria on or before the date of adoption
of the original Standards on September 4, 1974, shall
also be considered professional psychologists: (a) a
master's degree from a program primarily psychological in content from a regionally accredited university
or professional school; (b) appropriate education,
training, and experience in the area of service offered;
(c) a license or certificate in the state in which they
practice, conferred by a state board of psychological
examiners, or the endorsement of the state psychological association through voluntary certification, or,
for practice in primary and secondary schools, a state
department of education certificate as a school psychologist provided that the certificate required at least
two graduate years.

[5] Minutes of the Board of Professional Affairs
meeting, Washington, D.C., March 8–9, 1974.

[6] This definition is less restrictive than Recommendation 4 of the APA (1967) policy statement setting forth model state legislation affecting the practice of psychology (hereinafter referred to as State
Guidelines), proposing one level for state license or
certificate and "requiring the doctoral degree from an
accredited university or college in a program that is
primarily psychological, and no less than 2 years of
supervised experience, one of which is subsequent to

12   STANDARDS FOR PROVIDERS

the granting of the doctoral degree. This level should be designated by the title of 'psychologist' " (p. 1099).

The 1972 APA "Guidelines for Conditions of Employment of Psychologists" (hereinafter referred to as CEP Guidelines) introduces slightly different shadings of meaning in its section on "Standards for Entry into the Profession" as follows:

Persons are properly identified as psychologists when they have completed the training and experience recognized as necessary to perform functions consistent with one of the several levels in a career in psychology. This training includes possession of a degree earned in a program primarily psychological in content. In the case of psychological practice, it involves services for a fee, appropriate registration, certification, or licensing as provided by laws of the state in which the practices will apply. (APA, 1972, p. 331)

In some situations, specialty designations and standards may be relevant. *The National Register of Health Service Providers in Psychology*, which based its criteria on this standard, identifies qualified psychologists in the health services field.

[7] As noted in the opening section of these Standards, functions and activities of psychologists relating to the teaching of psychology, the writing or editing of scholarly or scientific manuscripts, and the conduct of scientific research do not fall within the purview of these Standards.

[8] These definitions should be compared to the State Guidelines, which include definitions of *psychologist* and the *practice of psychology* as follows:

A person represents himself to be a psychologist when he holds himself out to the public by any title or description of services incorporating the words "psychology," "psychological," "psychologist," and/or offers to render or renders services as defined below to individuals, groups, organizations, or the public for a fee, monetary or otherwise.

The practice of psychology within the meaning of this act is defined as rendering to individuals, groups or organizations, or the public any psychological service involving the application of principles, methods, and procedures of understanding, predicting, and influencing behavior, such as the principles pertaining to learning, perception, motivation, thinking, emotions, and interpersonal relationships; the methods and procedures of interviewing, counseling, and psychotherapy; of constructing, administering, and interpreting tests of mental abilities, aptitudes, interests, attitudes, personality characteristics, emotion, and motivation; and of assessing public opinion.

The application of said principles and methods includes but is not restricted to: diagnosis, prevention, and amelioration of adjustment problems and emotional and mental disorders of individuals and groups; hypnosis; educational and vocational counseling; personnel selection and management; the evaluation and planning for effective work and learning situations; advertising and market research; and the resolution of interpersonal and social conflicts.

Psychotherapy within the meaning of this act means the use of learning, conditioning methods, and emotional reactions, in a professional relationship, to assist a person or persons to modify feelings, attitudes, and behavior which are intellectually, socially, or emotionally maladjustive or ineffectual.

The practice of psychology shall be as defined above, any existing statute in the state of _____ to the contrary notwithstanding. (APA, 1967, pp. 1098–1099)

[9] The relation of a psychological service unit to a larger facility or institution is also addressed indirectly in the CEP Guidelines, which emphasize the roles, responsibilities, and prerogatives of the psychologist when he or she is employed by or provides services for another agency, institution, or business.

[10] This Standard replaces earlier recommendations in the 1967 State Guidelines concerning exemption of psychologists from licensure. Recommendations 8 and 9 of those Guidelines read as follows:

8. Persons employed as psychologists by accredited academic institutions, governmental agencies, research laboratories, and business corporations should be exempted, provided such employees are performing those duties for which they are employed by such organizations, and within the confines of such organizations.

9. Persons employed as psychologists by accredited academic institutions, governmental agencies, research laboratories, and business corporations consulting or offering their research findings or providing scientific information to like organizations for a fee should be exempted. (APA, 1967, p. 1100)

On the other hand, the 1967 State Guidelines specifically denied exemptions under certain conditions, as noted in Recommendations 10 and 11:

10. Persons employed as psychologists who offer or provide psychological services to the public for a fee, over and above the salary that they receive for the performance of their regular duties, should not be exempted.

11. Persons employed as psychologists by organizations that sell psychological services to the public should not be exempted. (APA, 1967, pp. 1100-1101)

The present APA policy, as reflected in this Standard, establishes a single code of practice for psychologists providing covered services to users in any setting. The present minimum requirement is that a psychologist providing any covered service must meet local statutory requirements for licensure or certification. See the section Principles and Implications of the Standards for an elaboration of this position.

[11] A closely related principle is found in the APA (1972) CEP Guidelines:

It is the policy of APA that psychology as an independent profession is entitled to parity with other health and human service professions in institutional practices and before the law. Psychologists in interdisciplinary settings such as colleges and universities, medical schools, clinics, private practice groups, and other agencies expect parity with other professions in such matters as academic rank, board status, salaries, fringe benefits, fees, participation in administrative decisions, and all other conditions of employment, private contractual arrangements, and status before the law and legal institutions. (APA, 1972, p. 333)

[12] See CEP Guidelines (section entitled "Career Development") for a closely related statement:

Psychologists are expected to encourage institutions and agencies which employ them to sponsor or conduct career development programs. The purpose of these programs would be to enable psychologists to engage in study for professional advancement and to keep abreast of developments in their field. (APA, 1972, p. 332)

[13] This Standard follows closely the statement regarding "Policy on Training for Psychologists Wishing to Change Their Specialty" adopted by the APA Council of Representatives in January 1976. Included therein was the implementing provision that "this policy statement shall be incorporated in the guidelines of the Committee on Accreditation so that appropriate sanctions can be brought to bear on university and internship training programs which violate [it]."

[14] See also APA's (1977) *Ethical Standards of Psychologists*, especially Principles 5 (Confidentiality), 6 (Welfare of the Consumer), and 9 (Pursuit of Research Activities); and see *Ethical Principles in the Conduct of Research with Human Participants* (APA, 1973a).

[15] Support for this position is found in the section in *Psychology as a Profession* on relations with other professions:

Professional persons have an obligation to know and take into account the traditions and practices of other professional groups with whom they work and to cooperate fully with members of such groups with whom research, service, and other functions are shared. (APA, 1968, p. 5)

[16] One example of a specific application of this principle is found in Guideline 2 in APA's (1973b) "Guidelines for Psychologists Conducting Growth Groups":

The following information should be made available *in writing* [italics added] to all prospective participants:

(a) An explicit statement of the purpose of the group;

(b) Types of techniques that may be employed;

(c) The education, training, and experience of the leader or leaders;

(d) The fee and any additional expense that may be incurred;

(e) A statement as to whether or not a follow-up service is included in the fee;

(f) Goals of the group experience and techniques to be used;

(g) Amounts and kinds of responsibility to be assumed by the leader and by the participants. For example, *(i)* the degree to which a participant is free not to follow suggestions and prescriptions of the group leader and other group members; *(ii)* any restrictions on a participant's freedom to leave the group at any time; and,

(h) Issues of confidentiality. (p. 933)

[17] See again Principle 5 (Confidentiality) in *Ethical Standards of Psychologists* (APA, 1977).

[18] Support for the principle of privileged communication is found in at least two policy statements of the Association:

In the interest of both the public and the client and in accordance with the requirements of good professional practice, the profession of psychology seeks recognition of the privileged nature of confidential communications with clients, preferably through statutory enactment or by administrative policy where more appropriate. (APA, 1968, p. 8)

25. Wherever possible, a clause protecting the privileged nature of the psychologist–client relationship be included.

26. When appropriate, psychologists assist in obtaining general "across the board" legislation for such privileged communications. (APA, 1967, p. 1103)

14   STANDARDS FOR PROVIDERS

[19] This paragraph is drawn directly from the CEP Guidelines (APA,.1972, p. 333).

[20] "It is recognized that under certain circumstances, the interests and goals of a particular community or segment of interest in the population may be in conflict with the general welfare. Under such circumstances, the psychologist's professional activity must be primarily guided by the principle of promoting human welfare." (APA, 1972, p. 334)

[21] Support for the principle of the independence of psychology as a profession is found in the following:

As a member of an autonomous profession, a psychologist rejects limitations upon his freedom of thought and action other than those imposed by his moral, legal, and social responsibilities. The Association is always prepared to provide appropriate assistance to any responsible member who becomes subjected to unreasonable limitations upon his opportunity to function as a practitioner, teacher, researcher, administrator, or consultant. The Association is always prepared to cooperate with any responsible professional organization in opposing any unreasonable limitations on the professional functions of the members of that organization.
This insistence upon professional autonomy has been upheld over the years by the affirmative actions of the courts and other public and private bodies in support of the right of the psychologist—and other professionals—to pursue those functions for which he is trained and qualified to perform. (APA, 1968, p. 9)

Organized psychology has the responsibility to define and develop its own profession, consistent with the general canons of science and with the public welfare.
Psychologists recognize that other professions and other groups will, from time to time, seek to define the roles and responsibilities of psychologists. The APA opposes such developments on the same principles that it is opposed to the psychological profession taking positions which would define the work and scope of responsibility of other duly recognized professions. . . . (APA, 1972, p. 333)

[22] APA support for peer review is detailed in the following excerpt from the APA (1971) statement entitled "Psychology and National Health Care":

All professions participating in a national health plan should be directed to establish review mechanisms (or performance evaluations) that include not only peer review but active participation by persons representing the consumer. In situations where there are fiscal agents, they should also have representation when appropriate. (p. 1026)

[23] This Standard on program evaluation is based directly on the following excerpts of two APA position papers:

The quality and availability of health services should be evaluated continuously by both consumers and health professionals. Research into the efficiency and effectiveness of the system should be conducted both internally and under independent auspices. (APA, 1971, p. 1025)

The comprehensive community mental health center should devote an explicit portion of its budget to program evaluation. All centers should inculcate in their staff attention to and respect for research findings; the larger centers have an obligation to set a high priority on basic research and to give formal recognition to research as a legitimate part of the duties of staff members.
. . . Only through explicit appraisal of program effects can worthy approaches be retained and refined, ineffective ones dropped. Evaluative monitoring of program achievements may vary, of course, from the relatively informal to the systematic and quantitative, depending on the importance of the issue, the availability of resources, and the willingness of those responsible to take the risks of substituting informed judgment for evidence. (Smith & Hobbs, 1966, pp. 21–22)

[24] See also the CEP Guidelines for the following statement: "A psychologist recognizes that . . . he alone is accountable for the consequences and effects of his services, whether as teacher, researcher, or practitioner. This responsibility cannot be shared, delegated, or reduced" (APA, 1972, p. 334).

REFERENCES

Accreditation Council for Facilities for the Mentally Retarded. *Standards for residential facilities for the mentally retarded.* Chicago, Ill.: Joint Commission on Accreditation of Hospitals, 1971.

American Psychological Association, Committee on Legislation. A model for state legislation affecting the practice of psychology 1967. *American Psychologist,* 1967, *22,* 1095–1103.

American Psychological Association. *Psychology as a profession.* Washington, D.C.: Author, 1968.

American Psychological Association. Psychology and national health care. *American Psychologist,* 1971, *26,* 1025–1026.

American Psychological Association. Guidelines for conditions of employment of psychologists. *American Psychologist,* 1972, *27,* 331–334.

American Psychological Association. *Ethical principles in the conduct of research with human participants.* Washington, D.C.: Author, 1973. (a)

American Psychological Association. Guidelines for psychologists conducting growth groups. *American Psychologist*, 1973, *28*, 933. (b)

American Psychological Association. *Standards for educational and psychological tests*. Washington, D.C.: Author, 1974.

American Psychological Association. *Ethical standards of psychologists* (Rev. ed.). Washington, D.C.: Author, 1977.

Joint Commission on Accreditation of Hospitals. *Accreditation manual for psychiatric facilities 1972*. Chicago, Ill.: Author, 1972.

Smith, M. B., & Hobbs, N. *The community and the community mental health center*. Washington, D.C.: American Psychological Association, 1966.

Appendix C:
Specialty Guidelines for
the Delivery of Services
by Counseling Psychologists

Specialty Guidelines for the Delivery of Services by Counseling Psychologists

The Specialty Guidelines that follow are based on the generic *Standards for Providers of Psychological Services* originally adopted by the American Psychological Association (APA) in September 1974 and revised in January 1977 (APA, 1974b, 1977b). Together with the generic *Standards*, these Specialty Guidelines state the official policy of the Association regarding delivery of services by counseling psychologists. Admission to the practice of psychology is regulated by state statute. It is the position of the Association that licensing be based on generic, and not on specialty, qualifications. Specialty guidelines serve the additional purpose of providing potential users and other interested groups with essential information about particular services available from the several specialties in professional psychology.

Professional psychology specialties have evolved from generic practice in psychology and are supported by university training programs. There are now at least four recognized professional specialties—clinical, counseling, school, and industrial/organizational psychology.

The knowledge base in each of these specialty areas has increased, refining the state of the art to the point that a set of uniform specialty guidelines is now possible and desirable. The present Guidelines are intended to educate the public, the profession, and other interested parties regarding specialty professional practices. They are also intended to facilitate the continued systematic development of the profession.

The content of each Specialty Guideline reflects a consensus of university faculty and public and private practitioners regarding the knowledge base, services provided, problems addressed, and clients served.

Traditionally, all learned disciplines have treated the designation of specialty practice as a reflection of preparation in greater depth in a particular subject matter, together with a voluntary limiting of focus to a more restricted area of practice by the professional. Lack of specialty designation does not preclude general providers of psychological services from using the methods or dealing with the populations of any specialty, except insofar as psychologists voluntarily refrain from providing services they are not trained to render. It is the intent of these guidelines, however, that after the grandparenting period, psychologists not put themselves forward as *specialists* in a given area of practice unless they meet the qualifications noted in the Guidelines (see Definitions). Therefore, these Guidelines are meant to apply only to those psychologists who voluntarily wish to be designated as *counseling psychologists*. They do not apply to other psychologists.

These Guidelines represent the profession's best judg-

ment of the conditions, credentials, and experience that contribute to competent professional practice. The APA strongly encourages, and plans to participate in, efforts to identify professional practitioner behaviors and job functions and to validate the relation between these and desired client outcomes. Thus, future revisions of these Guidelines will increasingly reflect the results of such efforts.

These Guidelines follow the format and, wherever applicable, the wording of the generic *Standards*.[1] (Note: Footnotes appear at the end of the Specialty Guidelines. See pp. 661–663.) The intent of these Guidelines is to improve the quality, effectiveness, and accessibility of psychological services. They are meant to provide guidance to providers, users, and sanctioners regarding best judgment of the profession on these matters. Although the Specialty Guidelines have been derived from and are consistent with the generic *Standards*, they may be used as separate documents. However, *Standards for Providers of Psychological Services* (APA, 1977b) shall remain the basic policy statement and shall take precedence where there are questions of interpretation.

Professional psychology in general and counseling psychology as a specialty have labored long and diligently to codify a uniform set of guidelines for the delivery of services by counseling psychologists that would serve the respective needs of users, providers, third-party purchasers, and sanctioners of psychological services.

The Committee on Professional Standards, established by the APA in January 1980, is charged with keeping the generic *Standards* and the Specialty Guidelines responsive to the needs of the public and the profession. It is also charged with continually reviewing, modifying, and extending them progressively as the profession and the science of psychology develop new knowledge, improved methods, and additional modes of psychological services.

The Specialty Guidelines for the Delivery of Services by Counseling Psychologists that follow have been established by the APA as a means of self-regulation to protect the public interest. They guide the specialty prac-

These Specialty Guidelines were prepared by the APA Committee on Standards for Providers of Psychological Services (COSPOPS), chaired by Durand F. Jacobs, with the advice of the officers and committee chairpersons of the Division of Counseling Psychology (Division 17). Barbara A. Kirk and Milton Schwebel served successively as the counseling psychology representative of COSPOPS, and Arthur Centor and Richard Kilburg were the Central Office liaisons to the committee. Norman Kagan, Samuel H. Osipow, Carl E. Thoresen, and Allen E. Ivey served successively as Division 17 presidents.

tice of counseling psychology by specifying important areas of quality assurance and performance that contribute to the goal of facilitating more effective human functioning.

Principles and Implications of the Specialty Guidelines

These Specialty Guidelines emerged from and reaffirm the same basic principles that guided the development of the generic *Standards for Providers of Psychological Services* (APA, 1977b):

1. These Guidelines recognize that admission to the practice of psychology is regulated by state statute.

2. It is the intention of the APA that the generic *Standards* provide appropriate guidelines for statutory licensing of psychologists. In addition, although it is the position of the APA that licensing be generic and not in specialty areas, these Specialty Guidelines in counseling psychology provide an authoritative reference for use in credentialing specialty providers of counseling psychological services by such groups as divisions of the APA and state associations and by boards and agencies that find such criteria useful for quality assurance.

3. A uniform set of Specialty Guidelines governs the quality of services to all users of counseling psychological services in both the private and the public sectors. Those receiving counseling psychological services are protected by the same kinds of safeguards, irrespective of sector; these include constitutional guarantees, statutory regulation, peer review, consultation, record review, and supervision.

4. A uniform set of Specialty Guidelines governs counseling psychological service functions offered by counseling psychologists, regardless of setting or form of remuneration. All counseling psychologists in professional practice recognize and are responsive to a uniform set of Specialty Guidelines, just as they are guided by a common code of ethics.

5. Counseling psychology Guidelines establish clear, minimally acceptable levels of quality for covered counseling psychological service functions, regardless of the nature of the users, purchasers, or sanctioners of such covered functions.

6. All persons providing counseling psychological services meet specified levels of training and experience that are consistent with, and appropriate to, the functions they perform. Counseling psychological services provided by persons who do not meet the APA qualifications for a professional counseling psychologist (see Definitions) are supervised by a professional counseling psychologist. Final responsibility and accountability for services provided rest with professional counseling psychologists.

7. When providing any of the covered counseling psychological service functions at any time and in any setting, whether public or private, profit or nonprofit, counseling psychologists observe these Guidelines in order to promote the best interests and welfare of the users

of such services. The extent to which counseling psychologists observe these Guidelines is judged by peers.

8. These Guidelines, while assuring the user of the counseling psychologist's accountability for the nature and quality of services specified in this document, do not preclude the counseling psychologist from using new methods or developing innovative procedures in the delivery of counseling services.

These Specialty Guidelines have broad implications both for users of counseling psychological services and for providers of such services:

1. Guidelines for counseling psychological services provide a foundation for mutual understanding between provider and user and facilitate more effective evaluation of services provided and outcomes achieved.

2. Guidelines for counseling psychologists are essential for uniformity in specialty credentialing of counseling psychologists.

3. Guidelines give specific content to the profession's concept of ethical practice as it applies to the functions of counseling psychologists.

4. Guidelines for counseling psychological services may have significant impact on tomorrow's education and training models for both professional and support personnel in counseling psychology.

5. Guidelines for the provision of counseling psychological services in human service facilities influence the determination of acceptable structure, budgeting, and staffing patterns in these facilities.

6. Guidelines for counseling psychological services require continual review and revision.

The Specialty Guidelines here presented are intended to improve the quality and delivery of counseling psychological services by specifying criteria for key aspects of the practice. Some settings may require additional and/or more stringent criteria for specific areas of service delivery.

Systematically applied, these Guidelines serve to establish a more effective and consistent basis for evaluating the performance of individual service providers as well as to guide the organization of counseling psychological service units in human service settings.

Definitions

Providers of counseling psychological services refers to two categories of persons who provide counseling psychological services:

A. Professional counseling psychologists.[2] Professional counseling psychologists have a doctoral degree from a regionally accredited university or professional school providing an organized, sequential counseling psychology program in an appropriate academic department in a university or college, or in an appropriate department or unit of a professional school. Counseling psychology programs that are accredited by the American Psychological Association are recognized as meeting the definition of a counseling psychology program. Counseling psychology programs that are not accredited by the American Psychological Association meet the definition of a counseling psychology program if they satisfy the following criteria:

1. The program is primarily psychological in nature and stands as a recognizable, coherent organizational entity within the institution.
2. The program provides an integrated, organized sequence of study.
3. The program has an identifiable body of students who are matriculated in that program for a degree.
4. There is a clear authority with primary responsibility for the core and specialty areas, whether or not the program cuts across administrative lines.
5. There is an identifiable psychology faculty, and a psychologist is responsible for the program.

The professional counseling psychologist's doctoral education and training experience[3] is defined by the institution offering the program. Only counseling psychologists, that is, those who meet the appropriate education and training requirements, have the minimum professional qualifications to provide unsupervised counseling psychological services. A professional counseling psychologist and others providing counseling psychological services under supervision (described below) form an integral part of a multilevel counseling psychological service delivery system.

B. All other persons who provide counseling psychological services under the supervision of a professional counseling psychologist. Although there may be variations in the titles of such persons, they are not referred to as counseling psychologists. Their functions may be indicated by use of the adjective *psychological* preceding the noun, for example, *psychological associate, psychological assistant, psychological technician,* or *psychological aide.*

Counseling psychological services refers to services provided by counseling psychologists that apply principles, methods, and procedures for facilitating effective functioning during the life-span developmental process.[4,5] In providing such services, counseling psychologists approach practice with a significant emphasis on positive aspects of growth and adjustment and with a developmental orientation. These services are intended to help persons acquire or alter personal–social skills, improve adaptability to changing life demands, enhance environmental coping skills, and develop a variety of problem-solving and decision-making capabilities. Counseling psychological services are used by individuals, couples, and families of all age groups to cope with problems connected with education, career choice, work, sex, marriage, family, other social relations, health, aging, and handicaps of a social or physical nature. The services are offered in such organizations as educational, rehabilitation, and health institutions and in a variety of other public and private agencies committed to service in one or more of the problem areas cited above. Counseling psychological services include the following:

A. Assessment, evaluation, and diagnosis. Procedures may include, but are not limited to, behavioral observation, interviewing, and administering and interpreting instruments for the assessment of educational achievement, academic skills, aptitudes, interests, cognitive abilities, attitudes, emotions, motivations, psychoneurological status, personality characteristics, or any other aspect of human experience and behavior that may contribute to understanding and helping the user.

B. Interventions with individuals and groups. Procedures include individual and group psychological counseling (e.g., education, career, couples, and family counseling) and may use a therapeutic, group process, or social-learning approach, or any other deemed to be appropriate. Interventions are used for purposes of prevention, remediation, and rehabilitation; they may incorporate a variety of psychological modalities, such as psychotherapy, behavior therapy, marital and family therapy, biofeedback techniques, and environmental design.

C. Professional consultation relating to A and B above, for example, in connection with developing in-service training for staff or assisting an educational institution or organization to design a plan to cope with persistent problems of its students.

D. Program development services in the areas of A, B, and C above, such as assisting a rehabilitation center to design a career-counseling program.

E. Supervision of all counseling psychological services, such as the review of assessment and intervention activities of staff.

F. Evaluation of all services noted in A through E above and research for the purpose of their improvement.

A *counseling psychological service unit* is the functional unit through which counseling psychological services are provided; such a unit may be part of a larger psychological service organization comprising psychologists of more than one specialty and headed by a professional psychologist:

A. A counseling psychological service unit provides predominantly counseling psychological services and is composed of one or more professional counseling psychologists and supporting staff.

B. A counseling psychological service unit may operate as a functional or geographic component of a larger multipsychological service unit or of a governmental, educational, correctional, health, training, industrial, or commercial organizational unit, or it may operate as an independent professional service.[6]

C. A counseling psychological service unit may take the form of one or more counseling psychologists providing professional services in a multidisciplinary setting.

D. A counseling psychological service unit may also take the form of a private practice, composed of one or more counseling psychologists serving individuals or groups, or the form of a psychological consulting firm serving organizations and institutions.

Users of counseling psychological services include:

A. Direct users or recipients of counseling psychological services.

B. Public and private institutions, facilities, or organizations receiving counseling psychological services.

C. Third-party purchasers—those who pay for the delivery of services but who are not the recipients of services.

D. Sanctioners—those who have a legitimate concern with the accessibility, timeliness, efficacy, and standards of quality attending the provision of counseling psychological services. Sanctioners may include members of the user's family, the court, the probation officer, the school administrator, the employer, the union representative, the facility director, and so on. Sanctioners may also include various governmental, peer review, and accreditation bodies concerned with the assurance of quality.

Guideline 1
PROVIDERS

1.1 *Each counseling psychological service unit offering psychological services has available at least one professional counseling psychologist and as many more professional counseling psychologists as are necessary to assure the adequacy and quality of services offered.*

INTERPRETATION: The intent of this Guideline is that one or more providers of psychological services in any counseling psychological service unit meet the levels of training and experience of the professional counseling psychologist as specified in the preceding definitions.[7]

When a professional counseling psychologist is not available on a full-time basis, the facility retains the services of one or more professional counseling psychologists on a regular part-time basis. The counseling psychologist so retained directs the psychological services, including supervision of the support staff, has the authority and participates sufficiently to assess the need for services, reviews the content of services provided, and assumes professional responsibility and accountability for them. The psychologist directing the service unit is responsible for determining and justifying appropriate ratios of psychologists to users and psychologists to support staff, in order to ensure proper scope, accessibility, and quality of services provided in that setting.

1.2 *Providers of counseling psychological services who do not meet the requirements for the professional counseling psychologist are supervised directly by a professional counseling psychologist who assumes professional responsibility and accountability for the services provided. The level and extent of supervision may vary from task to task so long as the supervising psychologist retains a sufficiently close supervisory relationship to meet this Guideline. Special proficiency training or supervision may be provided by a professional psycholo-*

gist of another specialty or by a professional from another discipline whose competence in the given area has been demonstrated by previous training and experience.

INTERPRETATION: In each counseling psychological service unit there may be varying levels of responsibility with respect to the nature and quality of services provided. Support personnel are considered to be responsible for their functions and behavior when assisting in the provision of counseling psychological services and are accountable to the professional counseling psychologist. Ultimate professional responsibility and accountability for the services provided require that the supervisor review reports and test protocols, and review and discuss intervention plans, strategies, and outcomes. Therefore, the supervision of all counseling psychological services is provided directly by a professional counseling psychologist in a face-to-face arrangement involving individual and/or group supervision. The extent of supervision is determined by the needs of the providers, but in no event is it less than 1 hour per week for each support staff member providing counseling psychological services.

To facilitate the effectiveness of the psychological service unit, the nature of the supervisory relationship is communicated to support personnel in writing. Such communications delineate the duties of the employees, describing the range and type of services to be provided. The limits of independent action and decision making are defined. The description of responsibility specifies the means by which the employee will contact the professional counseling psychologist in the event of emergency or crisis situations.

1.3 *Wherever a counseling psychological service unit exists, a professional counseling psychologist is responsible for planning, directing, and reviewing the provision of counseling psychological services. Whenever the counseling psychological service unit is part of a larger professional psychological service encompassing various psychological specialties, a professional psychologist shall be the administrative head of the service.*

INTERPRETATION: The counseling psychologist who directs or coordinates the unit is expected to maintain an ongoing or periodic review of the adequacy of services and to formulate plans in accordance with the results of such evaluation. He or she coordinates the activities of the counseling psychology unit with other professional, administrative, and technical groups, both within and outside the institution or agency. The counseling psychologist has related responsibilities including, but not limited to, directing the training and research activities of the service, maintaining a high level of professional and ethical practice, and ensuring that staff members function only within the areas of their competency.

To facilitate the effectiveness of counseling services by raising the level of staff sensitivity and professional -

skills, the counseling psychologist designated as director is responsible for participating in the selection of staff and support personnel whose qualifications and skills (e.g., language, cultural and experiential background, race, sex, and age) are relevant to the needs and characteristics of the users served.

1.4 *When functioning as part of an organizational setting, professional counseling psychologists bring their backgrounds and skills to bear on the goals of the organization, whenever appropriate, by participation in the planning and development of overall services.*[8]

INTERPRETATION: Professional counseling psychologists participate in the maintenance of high professional standards by representation on committees concerned with service delivery.

As appropriate to the setting, their activities may include active participation, as voting and as office-holding members, on the facility's professional staff and on other executive, planning, and evaluation boards and committees.

1.5 *Counseling psychologists maintain current knowledge of scientific and professional developments to preserve and enhance their professional competence.*

INTERPRETATION: Methods through which knowledge of scientific and professional developments may be gained include, but are not limited to, reading scientific and professional publications, attendance at professional workshops and meetings, participation in staff development programs, and other forms of continuing education.[9] The counseling psychologist has ready access to reference material related to the provision of psychological services. Counseling psychologists are prepared to show evidence periodically that they are staying abreast of current knowledge and practices in the field of counseling psychology through continuing education.

1.6 *Counseling psychologists limit their practice to their demonstrated areas of professional competence.*

INTERPRETATION: Counseling psychological services are offered in accordance with the providers' areas of competence as defined by verifiable training and experience. When extending services beyond the range of their usual practice, counseling psychologists obtain pertinent training or appropriate professional supervision. Such training or supervision is consistent with the extension of functions performed and services provided. An extension of services may involve a change in the theoretical orientation of the counseling psychologist, in the modality or techniques used, in the type of client, or in the kinds of problems or disorders for which services are to be provided.

1.7 *Professional psychologists who wish to qualify as counseling psychologists meet the same requirements*

with respect to subject matter and professional skills that apply to doctoral education and training in counseling psychology.[10]

INTERPRETATION: Education of doctoral-level psychologists to qualify them for specialty practice in counseling psychology is under the auspices of a department in a regionally accredited university or of a professional school that offers the doctoral degree in counseling psychology. Such education is individualized, with due credit being given for relevant course work and other requirements that have previously been satisfied. In addition, doctoral-level training supervised by a counseling psychologist is required. Merely taking an internship in counseling psychology or acquiring experience in a practicum setting is not adequate preparation for becoming a counseling psychologist when prior education has not been in that area. Fulfillment of such an individualized educational program is attested to by the awarding of a certificate by the supervising department or professional school that indicates the successful completion of preparation in counseling psychology.

1.8 *Professional counseling psychologists are encouraged to develop innovative theories and procedures and to provide appropriate theoretical and/or empirical support for their innovations.*

INTERPRETATION: A specialty of a profession rooted in a science intends continually to explore and experiment with a view to developing and verifying new and improved ways of serving the public and documents its innovations.

Guideline 2
PROGRAMS

2.1 *Composition and organization of a counseling psychological service unit:*

2.1.1 *The composition and programs of a counseling psychological service unit are responsive to the needs of the persons or settings served.*

INTERPRETATION: A counseling psychological service unit is structured so as to facilitate effective and economical delivery of services. For example, a counseling psychological service unit serving predominantly a low-income, ethnic, or racial minority group has a staffing pattern and service programs that are adapted to the linguistic, experiential, and attitudinal characteristics of the users.

2.1.2 *A description of the organization of the counseling psychological service unit and its lines of responsibility and accountability for the delivery of psychological services is available in written form to* staff of the unit and to users and sanctioners upon request.

INTERPRETATION: The description includes lines of responsibility, supervisory relationships, and the level and extent of accountability for each person who provides psychological services.

2.1.3 *A counseling psychological service unit includes sufficient numbers of professional and support personnel to achieve its goals, objectives, and purposes.*

INTERPRETATION: The work load and diversity of psychological services required and the specific goals and objectives of the setting determine the numbers and qualifications of professional and support personnel in the counseling psychological service unit. Where shortages in personnel exist, so that psychological services cannot be rendered in a professional manner, the director of the counseling psychological service unit initiates action to remedy such shortages. When this fails, the director appropriately modifies the scope or work load of the unit to maintain the quality of the services rendered and, at the same time, makes continued efforts to devise alternative systems for delivery of services.

2.2 *Policies:*

2.2.1 *When the counseling psychological service unit is composed of more than one person or is a component of a larger organization, a written statement of its objectives and scope of services is developed, maintained, and reviewed.*

INTERPRETATION: The counseling psychological service unit reviews its objectives and scope of services annually and revises them as necessary to ensure that the psychological services offered are consistent with staff competencies and current psychological knowledge and practice. This statement is discussed with staff, reviewed with the appropriate administrator, and distributed to users and sanctioners upon request, whenever appropriate.

2.2.2 *All providers within a counseling psychological service unit support the legal and civil rights of the users.*[11]

INTERPRETATION: Providers of counseling psychological services safeguard the interests of the users with regard to personal, legal, and civil rights. They are continually sensitive to the issue of confidentiality of information, the short-term and long-term impacts of their decisions and recommendations, and other matters pertaining to individual, legal, and civil rights. Concerns regarding the safeguarding of individual rights of users include, but are not limited to, problems of access to professional records in educational institutions, self-incrimination in judicial proceedings, involuntary commitment to hos-

pitals, protection of minors or legal incompetents, discriminatory practices in employment selection procedures, recommendation for special education provisions, information relative to adverse personnel actions in the armed services, and adjudication of domestic relations disputes in divorce and custodial proceedings. Providers of counseling psychological services take affirmative action by making themselves available to local committees, review boards, and similar advisory groups established to safeguard the human, civil, and legal rights of service users.

2.2.3 *All providers within a counseling psychological service unit are familiar with and adhere to the American Psychological Association's Standards for Providers of Psychological Services, Ethical Principles of Psychologists, Standards for Educational and Psychological Tests, Ethical Principles in the Conduct of Research With Human Participants, and other official policy statements relevant to standards for professional services issued by the Association.*

INTERPRETATION: Providers of counseling psychological services maintain current knowledge of relevant standards of the American Psychological Association.

2.2.4 *All providers within a counseling psychological service unit conform to relevant statutes established by federal, state, and local governments.*

INTERPRETATION: All providers of counseling psychological services are familiar with and conform to appropriate statutes regulating the practice of psychology. They also observe agency regulations that have the force of law and that relate to the delivery of psychological services (e.g., evaluation for disability retirement and special education placements). In addition, all providers are cognizant that federal agencies such as the Veterans Administration, the Department of Education, and the Department of Health and Human Services have policy statements regarding psychological services. Providers are familiar as well with other statutes and regulations, including those addressed to the civil and legal rights of users (e.g., those promulgated by the federal Equal Employment Opportunity Commission), that are pertinent to their scope of practice.

It is the responsibility of the American Psychological Association to maintain current files of those federal policies, statutes, and regulations relating to this section and to assist its members in obtaining them. The state psychological associations and the state licensing boards periodically publish and distribute appropriate state statutes and regulations, and these are on file in the counseling psychological service unit or the larger multipsychological service unit of which it is a part.

2.2.5 *All providers within a counseling psychological service unit inform themselves about and use the* network of human services in their communities in order to link users with relevant services and resources.

INTERPRETATION: Counseling psychologists and support staff are sensitive to the broader context of human needs. In recognizing the matrix of personal and social problems, providers make available to clients information regarding human services such as legal aid societies, social services, employment agencies, health resources, and educational and recreational facilities. Providers of counseling psychological services refer to such community resources and, when indicated, actively intervene on behalf of the users.

Community resources include the private as well as the public sectors. Consultation is sought or referral made within the public or private network of services whenever required in the best interest of the users. Counseling psychologists, in either the private or the public setting, utilize other resources in the community whenever indicated because of limitations within the psychological service unit providing the services. Professional counseling psychologists in private practice know the types of services offered through local community mental health clinics and centers, through family-service, career, and placement agencies, and through reading and other educational improvement centers and know the costs and the eligibility requirements for those services.

2.2.6 *In the delivery of counseling psychological services, the providers maintain a cooperative relationship with colleagues and co-workers in the best interest of the users.[12]*

INTERPRETATION: Counseling psychologists recognize the areas of special competence of other professional psychologists and of professionals in other fields for either consultation or referral purposes. Providers of counseling psychological services make appropriate use of other professional, research, technical, and administrative resources to serve the best interests of users and establish and maintain cooperative arrangements with such other resources as required to meet the needs of users.

2.3 *Procedures:*

2.3.1 *Each counseling psychological service unit is guided by a set of procedural guidelines for the delivery of psychological services.*

INTERPRETATION: Providers are prepared to provide a statement of procedural guidelines, in either oral or written form, in terms that can be understood by users, including sanctioners and local administrators. This statement describes the current methods, forms, procedures, and techniques being used to achieve the objectives and goals for psychological services.

2.3.2 *Providers of counseling psychological services develop plans appropriate to the providers' profes-*

sional practices and to the problems presented by the users.

INTERPRETATION: A counseling psychologist, after initial assessment, develops a plan describing the objectives of the psychological services and the manner in which they will be provided.[13] To illustrate, the agreement spells out the objective (e.g., a career decision), the method (e.g., short-term counseling), the roles (e.g., active participation by the user as well as the provider), and the cost. This plan is in written form. It serves as a basis for obtaining understanding and concurrence from the user and for establishing accountability and provides a mechanism for subsequent peer review. This plan is, of course, modified as changing needs dictate.

A counseling psychologist who provides services as one member of a collaborative effort participates in the development, modification (if needed), and implementation of the overall service plan and provides for its periodic review.

2.3.3 *Accurate, current, and pertinent documentation of essential counseling psychological services provided is maintained.*

INTERPRETATION: Records kept of counseling psychological services include, but are not limited to, identifying data, dates of services, types of services, significant actions taken, and outcome at termination. Providers of counseling psychological services ensure that essential information concerning services rendered is recorded within a reasonable time following their completion.

2.3.4 *Each counseling psychological service unit follows an established record retention and disposition policy.*

INTERPRETATION: The policy on record retention and disposition conforms to state statutes or federal regulations where such are applicable. In the absence of such regulations, the policy is (a) that the full record be maintained intact for at least 4 years after the completion of planned services or after the date of last contact with the user, whichever is later; (b) that if a full record is not retained, a summary of the record be maintained for an additional 3 years; and (c) that the record may be disposed of no sooner than 7 years after the completion of planned services or after the date of last contact, whichever is later.

In the event of the death or incapacity of a counseling psychologist in independent practice, special procedures are necessary to ensure the continuity of active service to users and the proper safeguarding of records in accordance with this Guideline. Following approval by the affected user, it is appropriate for another counseling psychologist, acting under the auspices of the professional standards review committee (PSRC) of the state, to review the record with the user and recommend a course of action for continuing professional service, if needed. Depending on local circumstances, appropriate arrangements for record retention and disposition may also be recommended by the reviewing psychologist.

This Guideline has been designed to meet a variety of circumstances that may arise, often years after a set of psychological services has been completed. Increasingly, psychological records are being used in forensic matters, for peer review, and in response to requests from users, other professionals, and other legitimate parties requiring accurate information about the exact dates, nature, course, and outcome of a set of psychological services. The 4-year period for retention of the full record covers the period of either undergraduate or graduate study of most students in postsecondary educational institutions, and the 7-year period for retention of at least a summary of the record covers the period during which a previous user is most likely to return for counseling psychological services in an educational institution or other organization or agency.

2.3.5 *Providers of counseling psychological services maintain a system to protect confidentiality of their records.*[14]

INTERPRETATION: Counseling psychologists are responsible for maintaining the confidentiality of information about users of services, from whatever source derived. All persons supervised by counseling psychologists, including nonprofessional personnel and students, who have access to records of psychological services maintain this confidentiality as a condition of employment and/or supervision.

The counseling psychologist does not release confidential information, except with the written consent of the user directly involved or his or her legal representative. The only deviation from this rule is in the event of clear and imminent danger to, or involving, the user. Even after consent for release has been obtained, the counseling psychologist clearly identifies such information as confidential to the recipient of the information.[15] If directed otherwise by statute or regulations with the force of law or by court order, the psychologist seeks a resolution to the conflict that is both ethically and legally feasible and appropriate.

Users are informed in advance of any limits in the setting for maintenance of confidentiality of psychological information. For instance, counseling psychologists in agency, clinic, or hospital settings inform their clients that psychological information in a client's record may be available without the client's written consent to other members of the professional staff associated with service to the client. Similar limitations on confidentiality of psychological information may be present in certain educational, industrial, military, or other institutional settings, or in instances in which the user has waived confidentiality for purposes of third-party payment.

Users have the right to obtain information from their psychological records. However, the records are the property of the psychologist or the facility in which the psychologist works and are, therefore, the responsibility of the psychologist and subject to his or her control.

When the user's intention to waive confidentiality is judged by the professional counseling psychologist to be contrary to the user's best interests or to be in conflict with the user's civil and legal rights, it is the responsibility of the counseling psychologist to discuss the implications of releasing psychological information and to assist the user in limiting disclosure only to information required by the present circumstance.

Raw psychological data (e.g., questionnaire returns or test protocols) in which a user is identified are released only with the written consent of the user or his or her legal representative and released only to a person recognized by the counseling psychologist as qualified and competent to use the data.

Any use made of psychological reports, records, or data for research or training purposes is consistent with this Guideline. Additionally, providers of counseling psychological services comply with statutory confidentiality requirements and those embodied in the American Psychological Association's *Ethical Principles of Psychologists* (APA, 1981b).

Providers of counseling psychological services who use information about individuals that is stored in large computerized data banks are aware of the possible misuse of such data as well as the benefits and take necessary measures to ensure that such information is used in a socially responsible manner.

Guideline 3
ACCOUNTABILITY

3.1 *The promotion of human welfare is the primary principle guiding the professional activity of the counseling psychologist and the counseling psychological service unit.*

INTERPRETATION: Counseling psychologists provide services to users in a manner that is considerate, effective, economical, and humane. Counseling psychologists are responsible for making their services readily accessible to users in a manner that facilitates the users' freedom of choice.

Counseling psychologists are mindful of their accountability to the sanctioners of counseling psychological services and to the general public, provided that appropriate steps are taken to protect the confidentiality of the service relationship. In the pursuit of their professional activities, they aid in the conservation of human, material, and financial resources.

The counseling psychological service unit does not withhold services to a potential client on the basis of that user's race, color, religion, gender, sexual orientation, age, or national origin; nor does it provide services in a discriminatory or exploitative fashion. Counseling psychologists who find that psychological services are being provided in a manner that is discriminatory or exploitative to users and/or contrary to these Guidelines or to state or federal statutes take appropriate corrective action, which may include the refusal to provide services. When conflicts of interest arise, the counseling psychologist is guided in the resolution of differences by the principles set forth in the American Psychological Association's *Ethical Principles of Psychologists* (APA, 1981b) and "Guidelines for Conditions of Employment of Psychologists" (APA, 1972).[16]

Recognition is given to the following considerations in regard to the withholding of service: (a) the professional right of counseling psychologists to limit their practice to a specific category of users with whom they have achieved demonstrated competence (e.g., adolescents or families); (b) the right and responsibility of counseling psychologists to withhold an assessment procedure when not validly applicable; (c) the right and responsibility of counseling psychologists to withhold services in specific instances in which their own limitations or client characteristics might impair the quality of the services; (d) the obligation of counseling psychologists to seek to ameliorate through peer review, consultation, or other personal therapeutic procedures those factors that inhibit the provision of services to particular individuals; and (e) the obligation of counseling psychologists who withhold services to assist clients in obtaining services from other sources.[17]

3.2 *Counseling psychologists pursue their activities as members of the independent, autonomous profession of psychology.*[18]

INTERPRETATION. Counseling psychologists, as members of an independent profession, are responsible both to the public and to their peers through established review mechanisms. Counseling psychologists are aware of the implications of their activities for the profession as a whole. They seek to eliminate discriminatory practices instituted for self-serving purposes that are not in the interest of the users (e.g., arbitrary requirements for referral and supervision by another profession). They are cognizant of their responsibilities for the development of the profession, participate where possible in the training and career development of students and other providers, participate as appropriate in the training of paraprofessionals or other professionals, and integrate and supervise the implementation of their contributions within the structure established for delivering psychological services. Counseling psychologists facilitate the development of, and participate in, professional standards review mechanisms.[19]

Counseling psychologists seek to work with other professionals in a cooperative manner for the good of the users and the benefit of the general public. Counseling psychologists associated with multidisciplinary settings support the principle that members of each participating profession have equal rights and opportunities to share all privileges and responsibilities of full membership in human service facilities and to administer service programs in their respective areas of competence.

3.3 *There are periodic, systematic, and effective evaluations of counseling psychological services.*[20]

INTERPRETATION. When the counseling psychological service unit is a component of a larger organization, regular evaluation of progress in achieving goals is provided for in the service delivery plan, including consideration of the effectiveness of counseling psychological services relative to costs in terms of use of time and money and the availability of professional and support personnel.

Evaluation of the counseling psychological service delivery system is conducted internally and, when possible, under independent auspices as well. This evaluation includes an assessment of effectiveness (to determine what the service unit accomplished), efficiency (to determine the total costs of providing the services), continuity (to ensure that the services are appropriately linked to other human services), availability (to determine appropriate levels and distribution of services and personnel), accessibility (to ensure that the services are barrier free to users), and adequacy (to determine whether the services meet the identified needs for such services).

There is a periodic reexamination of review mechanisms to ensure that these attempts at public safeguards are effective and cost efficient and do not place unnecessary encumbrances on the providers or impose unnecessary additional expenses on users or sanctioners for services rendered.

3.4 *Counseling psychologists are accountable for all aspects of the services they provide and are responsive to those concerned with these services.*[21]

INTERPRETATION. In recognizing their responsibilities to users, sanctioners, third-party purchasers, and other providers, and where appropriate and consistent with the users' legal rights and privileged communications, counseling psychologists make available information about, and provide opportunity to participate in, decisions concerning such issues as initiation, termination, continuation, modification, and evaluation of counseling psychological services.

Depending on the settings, accurate and full information is made available to prospective individual or organizational users regarding the qualifications of providers, the nature and extent of services offered, and where appropriate, financial and social costs.

Where appropriate, counseling psychologists inform users of their payment policies and their willingness to assist in obtaining reimbursement. To assist their users, those who accept reimbursement from a third party are acquainted with the appropriate statutes and regulations, the procedures for submitting claims, and the limits on confidentiality of claims information, in accordance with pertinent statutes.

Guideline 4
ENVIRONMENT

4.1 *Providers of counseling psychological services promote the development in the service setting of a physical, organizational, and social environment that facilitates optimal human functioning.*

INTERPRETATION: Federal, state, and local requirements for safety, health, and sanitation are observed.

As providers of services, counseling psychologists are concerned with the environment of their service unit, especially as it affects the quality of service, but also as it impinges on human functioning in the larger context. Physical arrangements and organizational policies and procedures are conducive to the human dignity, self-respect, and optimal functioning of users and to the effective delivery of service. Attention is given to the comfort and the privacy of providers and users. The atmosphere in which counseling psychological services are rendered is appropriate to the service and to the users, whether in an office, clinic, school, college, university, hospital, industrial organization, or other institutional setting.

FOOTNOTES

[1] The footnotes appended to these Specialty Guidelines represent an attempt to provide a coherent context of other policy statements of the Association regarding professional practice. The Guidelines extend these previous policy statements where necessary to reflect current concerns of the public and the profession.

[2] The following two categories of professional psychologists who met the criteria indicated below on or before the adoption of these Specialty Guidelines on January 31, 1980, are also considered counseling psychologists: Category 1—persons who completed (a) a doctoral degree program primarily psychological in content at a regionally accredited university or professional school and (b) 3 postdoctoral years of appropriate education, training, and experience in providing counseling psychological services as defined herein, including a minimum of 1 year in a counseling setting; Category 2—persons who on or before September 4, 1974, (a) completed a master's degree from a program primarily psychological in content at a regionally accredited university or professional school and (b) held a license or certificate in the state in which they practiced, conferred by a state board of psychological examiners, or the endorsement of the state psychological association through voluntary certification, and who, in addition, prior to January 31, 1980, (c) obtained 3 post-master's years of appropriate education, training, and experience in providing counseling psychological services as defined herein, including a minimum of 2 years in a counseling setting.

After January 31, 1980, professional psychologists who wish to be recognized as professional counseling psychologists are referred to Guideline 1.7.

[3] The areas of knowledge and training that are a part of the educational program for all professional psychologists have been presented in two APA documents, *Education and Credentialing in Psychology II* (APA, 1977a) and *Criteria for Accreditation of Doctoral Training Programs and Internships in Professional Psychology* (APA, 1979). There is consistency in the presentation of core areas in the education and training of all professional psychologists. The description of education and training in these Guidelines is based primarily on the document *Education and Credentialing in Psychology II*. It is intended to indicate broad areas of required curriculum, with the expectation that training programs will undoubtedly want to interpret the specific content of these areas in different ways depending on the nature, philosophy, and intent of the programs.

[4] Functions and activities of counseling psychologists relating to the teaching of psychology, the writing or editing of scholarly or scientific manuscripts, and the conduct of scientific research do not fall within the purview of these Guidelines.

[5] These definitions should be compared with the APA (1967) guidelines for state legislation (hereinafter referred to as state guidelines), which define *psychologist* (i.e., the generic professional psychologist, not the specialist counseling psychologist) and the *practice of psychology* as follows:

A person represents himself [or herself] to be a psychologist when he [or she] holds himself [or herself] out to the public by any title or description of services incorporating the words "psychology," "psychological," and/or offers to render or renders services as defined below to individuals, groups, organizations, or the public for a fee, monetary or otherwise.

The practice of psychology within the meaning of this act is defined as rendering to individuals, groups, organizations, or the public any psychological service involving the application of principles, methods, and procedures of understanding, predicting, and influencing behavior, such as the principles pertaining to learning, perception, motivation, thinking, emotions, and interpersonal relationships; the methods and procedures of interviewing, counseling, and psychotherapy; of constructing, administering, and interpreting tests of mental abilities, aptitudes, interests, attitudes, personality characteristics, emotion, and motivation; and of assessing public opinion.

The application of said principles and methods includes, but is not restricted to: diagnosis, prevention, and amelioration of adjustment problems and emotional and mental disorders of individuals and groups; hypnosis; educational and vocational counseling; personnel selection and management; the evaluation and planning for effective work and learning situations; advertising and market research; and the resolution of interpersonal and social conflicts.

Psychotherapy within the meaning of this act means the use of learning, conditioning methods, and emotional reactions, in a professional relationship, to assist a person or persons to modify feelings, attitudes, and behavior which are intellectually, socially, or emotionally maladjustive or ineffectual.

The practice of psychology shall be as defined above, any existing statute in the state of _____ to the contrary notwithstanding. (APA, 1967, pp. 1098–1099)

[6] The relation of a psychological service unit to a larger facility or institution is also addressed indirectly in the APA (1972)

"Guidelines for Conditions of Employment of Psychologists" (hereinafter referred to as CEP Guidelines), which emphasize the roles, responsibilities, and prerogatives of the psychologist when he or she is employed by or provides services for another agency, institution, or business.

[7] This Guideline replaces earlier recommendations in the 1967 state guidelines concerning exemption of psychologists from licensure. Recommendations 8 and 9 of those guidelines read as follows:

> Persons employed as psychologists by accredited academic institutions, governmental agencies, research laboratories, and business corporations should be exempted, provided such employees are performing those duties for which they are employed by such organizations, and within the confines of such organizations.
> Persons employed as psychologists by accredited academic institutions, governmental agencies, research laboratories, and business corporations consulting or offering their research findings or providing scientific information *to like organizations* for a fee should be exempted. (APA, 1967, p. 1100)

On the other hand, the 1967 state guidelines specifically denied exemptions under certain conditions, as noted in Recommendations 10 and 11:

> Persons employed as psychologists who offer or provide psychological services to the public for a fee, over and above the salary that they receive for the performance of their regular duties, should not be exempted.
> Persons employed as psychologists by organizations that sell psychological services to the public should not be exempted. (APA, 1967, pp. 1100–1101)

The present APA policy, as reflected in this Guideline, establishes a single code of practice for psychologists providing covered services to users in any setting. The present position is that a psychologist providing any covered service meets local statutory requirements for licensure or certification. See the section entitled Principles and Implications of the Specialty Guidelines for further elaboration of this point.

[8] A closely related principle is found in the APA (1972) CEP Guidelines:

> It is the policy of APA that psychology as an independent profession is entitled to parity with other health and human service professions in institutional practices and before the law. Psychologists in interdisciplinary settings such as colleges and universities, medical schools, clinics, private practice groups, and other agencies expect parity with other professions in such matters as academic rank, board status, salaries, fringe benefits, fees, participation in administrative decisions, and all other conditions of employment, private contractual arrangements, and status before the law and legal institutions. (APA, 1972, p. 333)

[9] See CEP Guidelines (section entitled Career Development) for a closely related statement:

> Psychologists are expected to encourage institutions and agencies which employ them to sponsor or conduct career development programs. The purpose of these programs would be to enable psychologists to engage in study for professional advancement and to keep abreast of developments in their field. (APA, 1972, p. 332)

[10] This Guideline follows closely the statement regarding "Policy on Training for Psychologists Wishing to Change Their Specialty" adopted by the APA Council of Representatives in January 1976. Included therein was the implementing provision

that "this policy statement shall be incorporated in the guidelines of the Committee on Accreditation so that appropriate sanctions can be brought to bear on university and internship training programs that violate [it]" (Conger, 1976, p. 424).

[11] See also APA's (1981b) *Ethical Principles of Psychologists*, especially Principles 5 (Confidentiality), 6 (Welfare of the Consumer), and 9 (Research With Human Participants); and see *Ethical Principles in the Conduct of Research With Human Participants* (APA, 1973a). Also, in 1978 Division 17 approved in principle a statement on "Principles for Counseling and Psychotherapy With Women," which was designed to protect the interests of female users of counseling psychological services.

[12] Support for this position is found in the section on relations with other professions in *Psychology as a Profession*:

> Professional persons have an obligation to know and take into account the traditions and practices of other professional groups with whom they work and to cooperate fully with members of such groups with whom research, service, and other functions are shared. (APA, 1968, p. 5)

[13] One example of a specific application of this principle is found in APA's (1981a) revised *APA/CHAMPUS Outpatient Psychological Provider Manual*. Another example, quoted below, is found in Guideline 2 in APA's (1973b) "Guidelines for Psychologists Conducting Growth Groups":

> The following information should be made available *in writing* [italics added] to all prospective participants:
> (a) An explicit statement of the purpose of the group;
> (b) Types of techniques that may be employed;
> (c) The education, training, and experience of the leader or leaders;
> (d) The fee and any additional expense that may be incurred;
> (e) A statement as to whether or not a follow-up service is included in the fee;
> (f) Goals of the group experience and techniques to be used;
> (g) Amounts and kinds of responsibility to be assumed by the leader and by the participants. For example, (i) the degree to which a participant is free not to follow suggestions and prescriptions of the group leader and other group members; (ii) any restrictions on a participant's freedom to leave the group at any time; and
> (h) Issues of confidentiality. (p. 933)

[14] See Principle 5 (Confidentiality) in *Ethical Principles of Psychologists* (APA, 1981b).

[15] Support for the principles of privileged communication is found in at least two policy statements of the Association:

> In the interest of both the public and the client and in accordance with the requirements of good professional practice, the profession of psychology seeks recognition of the privileged nature of confidential communications with clients, preferably through statutory enactment or by administrative policy where more appropriate. (APA, 1968, p. 8)

> Wherever possible, a clause protecting the privileged nature of the psychologist–client relationship be included.
> When appropriate, psychologists assist in obtaining general "across the board" legislation for such privileged communications. (APA, 1967, p. 1103)

[16] The CEP Guidelines include the following;

> It is recognized that under certain circumstances, the interests and goals of a particular community or segment of

interest in the population may be in conflict with the general welfare. Under such circumstances, the psychologist's professional activity must be primarily guided by the principle of "promoting human welfare." (APA, 1972, p. 334)

[17] This paragraph is adapted in part from the CEP Guidelines (APA, 1972, p. 333).

[18] Support for the principle of the independence of psychology as a profession is found in the following:

As a member of an autonomous profession, a psychologist rejects limitations upon his [or her] freedom of thought and action other than those imposed by his [or her] moral, legal, and social responsibilities. The Association is always prepared to provide appropriate assistance to any responsible member who becomes subjected to unreasonable limitations upon his [or her] opportunity to function as a practitioner, teacher, researcher, administrator, or consultant. The Association is always prepared to cooperate with any responsible professional organization in opposing any unreasonable limitations on the professional functions of the members of that organization.

This insistence upon professional autonomy has been upheld over the years by the affirmative actions of the courts and other public and private bodies in support of the right of the psychologist—and other professionals—to pursue those functions for which he [or she] is trained and qualified to perform. (APA, 1968, p. 9)

Organized psychology has the responsibility to define and develop its own profession, consistent with the general canons of science and with the public welfare.

Psychologists recognize that other professions and other groups will, from time to time, seek to define the roles and responsibilities of psychologists. The APA opposes such developments on the same principle that it is opposed to the psychological profession taking positions which would define the work and scope of responsibility of other duly recognized professions. (APA, 1972, p. 333)

[19] APA support for peer review is detailed in the following excerpt from the APA (1971) statement entitled "Psychology and National Health Care":

All professions participating in a national health plan should be directed to establish review mechanisms (or performance evaluations) that include not only peer review but active participation by persons representing the consumer. In situations where there are fiscal agents, they should also have representation when appropriate. (p. 1026)

[20] This Guideline on program evaluation is based directly on the following excerpts from two APA position papers:

The quality and availability of health services should be evaluated continuously by both consumers and health professionals. Research into the efficiency and effectiveness of the system should be conducted both internally and under independent auspices. (APA, 1971, p. 1025)

The comprehensive community mental health center should devote an explicit portion of its budget to program evaluation. All centers should inculcate in their staff attention to and respect for research findings; the larger centers have an obligation to set a high priority on basic research and to

give formal recognition to research as a legitimate part of the duties of staff members.

. . . Only through explicit appraisal of program effects can worthy approaches be retained and refined, ineffective ones dropped. Evaluative monitoring of program achievements may vary, of course, from the relatively informal to the systematic and quantitative, depending on the importance of the issue, the availability of resources, and the willingness of those responsible to take risks of substituting informed judgment for evidence. (Smith & Hobbs, 1966, pp. 21–22)

[21] See also the CEP Guidelines for the following statement: "A psychologist recognizes that . . . he [or she] alone is accountable for the consequences and effects of his [or her] services, whether as teacher, researcher, or practitioner. This responsibility cannot be shared, delegated, or reduced" (APA, 1972, p. 334).

REFERENCES

American Psychological Association, Committee on Legislation. A model for state legislation affecting the practice of psychology. *American Psychologist*, 1967, *22*, 1095–1103.

American Psychological Association. *Psychology as a profession*. Washington, D.C.: Author, 1968.

American Psychological Association. Psychology and national health care. *American Psychologist*, 1971, *26*, 1025–1026.

American Psychological Association. Guidelines for conditions of employment of psychologists. *American Psychologist*, 1972, *27*, 331–334.

American Psychological Association. *Ethical principles in the conduct of research with human participants*. Washington, D.C.: Author, 1973. (a)

American Psychological Association. Guidelines for psychologists conducting growth groups. *American Psychologist*, 1973, *28*, 933. (b)

American Psychological Association. *Standards for educational and psychological tests*. Washington, D.C.: Author, 1974. (a)

American Psychological Association. *Standards for providers of psychological services*. Washington, D.C.: Author, 1974. (b)

American Psychological Association. *Education and credentialing in psychology II*. Report of a meeting, June 4–5, 1977. Washington, D.C.: Author, 1977. (a)

American Psychological Association. *Standards for providers of psychological services* (Rev. ed.). Washington, D.C.: Author, 1977. (b)

American Psychological Association. *Criteria for accreditation of doctoral training programs and internships in professional psychology*. Washington, D.C.: Author, 1979 (amended 1980).

American Psychological Association. *APA/CHAMPUS outpatient psychological provider manual* (Rev. ed.). Washington, D.C.: Author, 1981. (a)

American Psychological Association. *Ethical principles of psychologists* (Rev. ed.). Washington, D.C.: Author, 1981. (b)

Conger, J. J. Proceedings of the American Psychological Association, Incorporated, for the year 1975: Minutes of the annual meeting of the Council of Representatives. *American Psychologist*, 1976, *31*, 406–434.

Smith, M. B., & Hobbs, N. *The community and the community mental health center*. Washington, D.C.: American Psychological Association, 1966.

Appendix D:
American Association for Counseling and Development Code of Ethics

American Association for Counseling and Development

PREAMBLE

The Association is an educational, scientific, and professional organization whose members are dedicated to the enhancement of the worth, dignity, potential, and uniqueness of each individual and thus to the service of society.

The Association recognizes that the role definitions and work settings of its members include a wide variety of academic disciplines, levels of academic preparation and agency services. This diversity reflects the breadth of the Association's interest and influence. It also poses challenging complexities in efforts to set standards for the performance of members, desired requisite preparation or practice, and supporting social, legal, and ethical controls.

The specification of ethical standards enables the Association to clarify to present and future members and to those served by members, the nature of ethical responsibilities held in common by its members.

The existence of such standards serves to stimulate greater concern by members for their own professional functioning and for the conduct of fellow professionals such as counselors, guidance and student personnel workers, and others in the helping professions. As the ethical code of the Association, this document establishes principles that define the ethical behavior of Association members.

Source: AACD Code of Ethics, approved by Executive Committee upon referral of the Board of Directors, January 17, 1981. Reprinted by permission of the American Association for Counseling and Development.

Note: A revision of the current AACD standards is currently in progress. New version to be released pending AACD approval.

SECTION A: GENERAL

1. The member influences the development of the profession by continuous efforts to improve professional practices, teaching, services, and research. Professional growth is continuous throughout the member's career and is exemplified by the development of a philosophy that explains why and how a member functions in the helping relationship. Members must gather data on their effectiveness and be guided by the findings.

2. The member has a responsibility both to the individual who is served and to the institution within which the service is performed to maintain high standards of professional conduct. The member strives to maintain the highest levels of professional services offered to the individuals to be served. The member also strives to assist the agency, organization, or institution in providing the highest caliber of professional services. The acceptance of employment in an institution implies that the member is in agreement with the general policies and principles of the institution. Therefore the professional activities of the member are also in accord with the objectives of the institution. If, despite concerted efforts, the member cannot reach agreement with the employer as to acceptable standards of conduct that allow for changes in institutional policy conducive to the positive growth and development of clients, then terminating the affiliation should be seriously considered.

3. Ethical behavior among professional associates, both members and nonmembers, must be expected at all times. When information is possessed that raises doubt as to the ethical behavior of professional colleagues, whether Association members or not, the member must take action to attempt to rectify such a condition. Such action shall use the institution's channels first and then use procedures established by the state Branch, Division, or Association.

4. The member neither claims nor implies professional qualifications exceeding those possessed and is responsible for correcting any misrepresentations of these qualifications by others.

5. In establishing fees for professional counseling services, members must consider the financial status of clients and locality. In the event that the established fee structure is inappropriate for a client, assistance must be provided in finding comparable services of acceptable cost.

6. When members provide information to the public or to subordinates, peers or supervisors, they have a responsibility to ensure

that the content is general, unidentified client information that is accurate, unbiased, and consists of objective, factual data.

7. With regard to the delivery of professional services, members should accept only those positions for which they are professionally qualified.

8. In the counseling relationship the counselor is aware of the intimacy of the relationship and maintains respect for the client and avoids engaging in activities that seek to meet the counselor's personal needs at the expense of that client. Through awareness of the negative impact of both racial and sexual stereotyping and discrimination, the counselor guards the individual rights and personal dignity of the client in the counseling relationship.

SECTION B: COUNSELING RELATIONSHIP

This section refers to practices and procedures of individual and/or group counseling relationships.

The member must recognize the need for client freedom of choice. Under those circumstances where this is not possible, the member must apprise clients of restrictions that may limit their freedom of choice.

1. The member's *primary* obligation is to respect the integrity and promote the welfare of the client(s), whether the client(s) is (are) assisted individually or in a group relationship. In a group setting, the member is also responsible for taking reasonable precautions to protect individuals from physical and/or psychological trauma resulting from interaction within the group.

2. The counseling relationship and information resulting therefrom must be kept confidential, consistent with the obligations of the member as a professional person. In a group counseling setting, the counselor must set a norm of confidentiality regarding all group participants' disclosures.

3. If an individual is already in a counseling relationship with another professional person, the member does not enter into a counseling relationship without first contacting and receiving the approval of that other professional. If the member discovers that the client is in another counseling relationship after the counseling relationship begins, the member must gain the consent of the other professional or terminate the relationship, unless the client elects to terminate the other relationship.

4. When the client's condition indicates that there is clear and imminent danger to the client or others, the member must take reasonable personal action or inform responsible authorities. Consultation with other professionals must be used where possible. The assumption of responsibility for the client(s) behavior must be taken only after careful deliberation. The client must be involved in the resumption of responsibility as quickly as possible.

5. Records of the counseling relationship, including interview notes, test data, correspondence, tape recordings, and other documents, are to be considered professional information for use in counseling and they should not be considered a part of the records of the institution or agency in which the counselor is employed unless specified by state statute or regulation. Revelation to others of counseling material must occur only upon the expressed consent of the client.

6. Use of data derived from a counseling relationship for purposes of counselor training or research shall be confined to content that can be disguised to ensure full protection of the identity of the subject client.

7. The member must inform the client of the purposes, goals, techniques, rules of procedure and limitations that may affect the relationship at or before the time that the counseling relationship is entered.

8. The member must screen prospective group participants, especially when the emphasis is on self-understanding and growth through self-disclosure. The member must maintain an awareness of the group participants' compatibility throughout the life of the group.

9. The member may choose to consult with any other professionally competent person about a client. In choosing a consultant, the member must avoid placing the consultant in a conflict of interest situation that would preclude the consultant's being a proper party to the member's efforts to help the client.

10. If the member determines an inability to be of professional assistance to the client, the member must either avoid initiating the counseling relationship or immediately terminate that relationship. In either event, the member must suggest appropriate alternatives. (The member must be knowledgeable about referral resources so that a satisfactory referral can be initiated). In the event the client declines the suggested referral, the member is not obligated to continue the relationship.

11. When the member has other relationships, particularly of an administrative, supervisory and/or evaluative nature with an individual seeking counseling services, the member must not serve as the counselor but should refer the individual to another professional. Only in instances where such an alternative is unavailable and where the individual's situation warrants counseling intervention should the member enter into and/or maintain a counseling relationship. Dual relationships with clients that might impair the member's objectivity and professional judgment (e.g., as with close friends or relatives, sexual intimacies with any client) must be avoided and/or the counseling relationship terminated through referral to another competent professional.

12. All experimental methods of treatment must be clearly indicated to prospective recipients and safety precautions are to be adhered to by the member.

13. When the member is engaged in short-term group treatment/ training programs (e.g., marathons and other encounter-type or growth groups), the member ensures that there is professional assistance available during and following the group experience.

14. Should the member be engaged in a work setting that calls for any variation from the above statements, the member is obligated to consult with other professionals whenever possible to consider justifiable alternatives.

SECTION C: MEASUREMENT AND EVALUATION

The primary purpose of educational and psychological testing is to provide descriptive measures that are objective and interpretable in either comparative or absolute terms. The member must recognize the need to interpret the statements that follow as applying to the whole range of appraisal techniques including test and nontest data. Test results constitute only one of a variety of pertinent sources of information for personnel, guidance, and counseling decisions.

1. The member must provide specific orientation or information to the examinee(s) prior to and following the test administration so that the results of testing may be placed in proper perspective with other relevant factors. In so doing, the member must recognize the effects of socioeconomic, ethnic and cultural factors on test scores.

It is the member's professional responsibility to use additional un-validated information carefully in modifying interpretation of the test results.

2. In selecting tests for use in a given situation or with a particular client, the member must consider carefully the specific validity, reliability, and appropriateness of the test(s). *General* validity, reliability and the like may be questioned legally as well as ethically when tests are used for vocational and educational selection, placement, or counseling.

3. When making any statements to the public about tests and testing, the member must give accurate information and avoid false claims or misconceptions. Special efforts are often required to avoid unwarranted connotations of such terms as *IQ* and *grade equivalent scores.*

4. Different tests demand different levels of competence for administration, scoring, and interpretation. Members must recognize the limits of their competence and perform only those functions for which they are prepared.

5. Tests must be administered under the same conditions that were established in their standardization. When tests are not administered under standard conditions or when unusual behavior or irregularities occur during the testing session, those conditions must be noted and the results designated as invalid or of questionable validity. Unsupervised or inadequately supervised test-taking, such as the use of tests through the mails, is considered unethical. On the other hand, the use of instruments that are so designed or standardized to be self-administered and self-scored, such as interest inventories, is to be encouraged.

6. The meaningfulness of test results used in personnel, guidance, and counseling functions generally depends on the examinee's unfamiliarity with the specific items on the test. Any prior coaching or dissemination of the test materials can invalidate test results. Therefore, test security is one of the professional obligations of the member. Conditions that produce most favorable test results must be made known to the examinee.

7. The purpose of testing and the explicit use of the results must be made known to the examinee prior to testing. The counselor must ensure that instrument limitations are not exceeded and that periodic review and/or retesting are made to prevent client stereotyping.

8. The examinee's welfare and explicit prior understanding must be the criteria for determining the recipients of the test results. The

member must see that specific interpretation accompanies any release of individual or group test data. The interpretation of test data must be related to the examiner's particular concerns.

9. The member must be cautious when interpreting the results of research instruments possessing insufficient technical data. The specific purposes for the use of such instruments must be stated explicitly to examinees.

10. The member must proceed with caution when attempting to evaluate and interpret the performance of minority group members or other persons who are not represented in the norm group on which the instrument was standardized.

11. The member must guard against the appropriation, reproduction, or modifications of published tests or parts thereof without acknowledgment and permission from the previous publisher.

12. Regarding the preparation, publication and distribution of tests, reference should be made to:

a. *Standards for Educational and Psychological Tests and Manuals*, revised edition, 1974, published by the American Psychological Association on behalf of itself, the American Educational Research Association and the National Council on Measurement in Education.

b. The responsible use of tests: A position paper of AMEG, APGA, and NCME. *Measurement and Evaluation in Guidance*, 1972, 5, 385–388.

c. "Responsibilities of Users of Standardized Tests," APGA, *Guidepost*, October 5, 1978, pp. 5–8.

SECTION D: RESEARCH AND PUBLICATION

1. Guidelines on research with human subjects shall be adhered to, such as:

a. *Ethical Principles in the Conduct of Research with Human Participants*, Washington, D.C.: American Psychological Association, Inc., 1973.

b. Code of Federal Regulations, Title 45, Subtitle A, Part 46, as currently issued.

2. In planning any research activity dealing with human subjects, the member must be aware of and responsive to all pertinent ethical principles and ensure that the research problem, design, and execution are in full compliance with them.

3. Responsibility for ethical research practice lies with the principal researcher, while others involved in the research activities share ethical obligation and full responsibility for their own actions.

4. In research with human subjects, researchers are responsible for the subjects' welfare throughout the experiment and they must take all reasonable precautions to avoid causing injurious psychological, physical, or social effects on their subjects.

5. All research subjects must be informed of the purpose of the study except when withholding information or providing misinformation to them is essential to the investigation. In such research the member must be responsible for corrective action as soon as possible following completion of the research.

6. Participation in research must be voluntary. Involuntary participation is appropriate only when it can be demonstrated that participation will have no harmful effects on subjects and is essential to the investigation.

7. When reporting research results, explicit mention must be made of all variables and conditions known to the investigator that might affect the outcome of the investigation or the interpretation of the data.

8. The member must be responsible for conducting and reporting investigations in a manner that minimizes the possibility that results will be misleading.

9. The member has an obligation to make available sufficient original research data to qualified others who may wish to replicate the study.

10. When supplying data, aiding in the research of another person, reporting research results, or in making original data available, due care must be taken to disguise the identity of the subjects in the absence of specific authorization from such subjects to do otherwise.

11. When conducting and reporting research, the member must be familiar with, and give recognition to, previous work on the topic, as well as to observe all copyright laws and follow the principles of giving full credit to all to whom credit is due.

12. The member must give due credit through joint authorship, acknowledgment, footnote statements, or other appropriate means to those who have contributed significantly to the research and/or publication, in accordance with such contributions.

13. The member must communicate to other members the results of any research judged to be of professional or scientific value.

Results reflecting unfavorably on institutions, programs, services, or vested interests must not be withheld for such reasons.

14. If members agree to cooperate with another individual in research and/or publication, they incur an obligation to cooperate as promised in terms of punctuality of performance and with full regard to the completeness and accuracy of the information required.

15. Ethical practice requires that authors not submit the same manuscript or one essentially similar in content, for simultaneous publication consideration by two or more journals. In addition, manuscripts published in whole or in substantial part, in another journal or published work should not be submitted for publication without acknowledgment and permission from the previous publication.

SECTION E: CONSULTING

Consultation refers to a voluntary relationship between a professional helper and help-needing individual, group or social unit in which the consultant is providing help to the client(s) in defining and solving a work-related problem or potential problem with a client or client system. (This definition is adapted from Kurpius, DeWayne. Consultation theory and process: An integrated model. *Personnel and Guidance Journal,* 1978, 56.)

1. The member acting as consultant must have a high degree of self-awareness of his/her own values, knowledge, skills, limitations, and needs in entering a helping relationship that involves human and/or organizational change and that the focus of the relationship be on the issues to be resolved and not on the person(s) presenting the problem.

2. There must be understanding and agreement between member and client for the problem definition, change goals, and predicated consequences of interventions selected.

3. The member must be reasonably certain that she/he or the organization represented has the necessary competencies and resources for giving the kind of help that is needed now or may develop later and that appropriate referral resources are available to the consultant.

4. The consulting relationship must be one in which client adaptability and growth toward self-direction are encouraged and

cultivated. The member must maintain this role consistently and not become a decision maker for the client or create a future dependency on the consultant.

5. When announcing consultant availability for services, the member conscientiously adheres to the Association's *Ethical Standards*.

6. The member must refuse a private fee or other remuneration for consultation with persons who are entitled to these services through the member's employing institution or agency. The policies of a particular agency may make explicit provisions for private practice with agency clients by members of its staff. In such instances, the clients must be apprised of other options open to them should they seek private counseling services.

SECTION F: PRIVATE PRACTICE

1. The member should assist the profession by facilitating the availability of counseling services in private as well as public settings.

2. In advertising services as a private practitioner, the member must advertise the services in such a manner so as to accurately inform the public as to services, expertise, profession, and techniques of counseling in a professional manner. A member who assumes an executive leadership role in the organization shall not permit his/her name to be used in professional notices during periods when not actively engaged in the private practice of counseling.

The member may list the following: highest relevant degree, type and level of certification or license, type and/or description of services, and other relevant information. Such information must not contain false, inaccurate, misleading, partial, out-of-context, or deceptive material or statements.

3. Members may join in partnership/corporation with other members and/or other professionals provided that each member of the partnership or corporation makes clear the separate specialties by name in compliance with the regulations of the locality.

4. A member has an obligation to withdraw from a counseling relationship if it is believed that employment will result in violation of the *Ethical Standards*. If the mental or physical condition of the member renders it difficult to carry out an effective professional relationship or if the member is discharged by the client because the

counseling relationship is no longer productive for the client, then the member is obligated to terminate the counseling relationship.

5. A member must adhere to the regulations for private practice of the locality where the services are offered.

6. It is unethical to use one's institutional affiliation to recruit clients for one's private practice.

SECTION G: PERSONNEL ADMINISTRATION

It is recognized that most members are employed in public or quasi-public institutions. The functioning of a member within an institution must contribute to the goals of the institution and vice versa if either is to accomplish their respective goals or objectives. It is therefore essential that the member and the institution function in ways to (a) make the institution's goals explicit and public; (b) make the member's contribution to institutional goals specific; and (c) foster mutual accountability for goal achievement.

To accomplish these objectives, it is recognized that the member and the employer must share responsibilities in the formulation and implementation of personnel policies.

1. Members must define and describe the parameters and levels of their professional competency.

2. Members must establish interpersonal relations and working agreements with supervisors and subordinates regarding counseling or clinical relationships, confidentiality, distinction between public and private material, maintenance, and dissemination of recorded information, work load and accountability. Working agreements in each instance must be specified and made known to those concerned.

3. Members must alert their employers to conditions that may be potentially disruptive or damaging.

4. Members must inform employers of conditions that may limit their effectiveness.

5. Members must submit regularly to professional review and evaluation.

6. Members must be responsible for inservice development of self and/or staff.

7. Members must inform their staff of goals and programs.

8. Members must provide personnel practices that guarantee and enhance the rights and welfare of each recipient of their service.

9. Members must select competent persons and assign responsibilities compatible with their skills and experiences.

SECTION H: PREPARATION STANDARDS

Members who are responsible for training others must be guided by the preparation standards of the Association and relevant Division(s). The member who functions in the capacity of trainer assumes unique ethical responsibilities that frequently go beyond that of the member who does not function in a training capacity. These ethical responsibilities are outlined as follows:

1. Members must orient students to program expectations, basic skills development and employment prospects prior to admission to the program.

2. Members in charge of learning experiences must establish programs that integrate academic study and supervised practice.

3. Members must establish a program directed toward developing students' skills, knowledge, and self-understanding, stated whenever possible in competency or performance terms.

4. Members must identify the levels of competencies of their students in compliance with relevant Division standards. These competencies must accommodate the para-professional as well as the professional.

5. Members, through continual student evaluation and appraisal, must be aware of the personal limitations of the learner that might impede future performance. The instructor must not only assist the learner in securing remedial assistance but also screen from the program those individuals who are unable to provide competent services.

6. Members must provide a program that includes training in research commensurate with levels of role functioning. Para-professional and technician-level personnel must be trained as consumers of research. In addition, these personnel must learn how to evaluate their own and their program's effectiveness. Graduate training, especially at the doctoral level, would include preparation for original research by the member.

7. Members must make students aware of the ethical responsibilities and standards of the profession.

8. Preparatory programs must encourage students to value the ideals of service to individuals and to society. In this regard, direct

financial remuneration or lack thereof must not influence the quality of service rendered. Monetary considerations must not be allowed to overshadow professional and humanitarian needs.

9. Members responsible for educational programs must be skilled as teachers and practitioners.

10. Members must present thoroughly varied theoretical positions so that students may make comparisons and have the opportunity to select a position.

11. Members must develop clear policies within their educational institutions regarding field placement and the roles of the student and the instructor in such placements.

12. Members must ensure that forms of learning focusing on self-understanding or growth are voluntary, or if required as part of the education program, are made known to prospective students prior to entering the program. When the education program offers a growth experience with an emphasis on self-disclosure or other relatively intimate or personal involvement, the member must have no administrative, supervisory, or evaluating authority regarding the participant.

13. Members must conduct an educational program in keeping with the current relevant guidelines of the Association and its Divisions.

Index

Index